M000273538

KINGDOM *Sparkle*

Twelve Gifts for a Radiant Life

KIMBERLY MOORE

parkcities
PUBLISHING

Kingdom Sparkle
Twelve Gifts for a Radiant Life

Published in Dallas, Texas by Park Cities Publishing.

Affiliated website: www.kingdomsparkle.com

Design and layout: Kathrine Tripp
Jewelry photographer: Cyndi Long

ISBN 978-0-578-71902-3

Printed in the United States of America.

Dedication

To my dear friends who are like precious gems.
You add so much sparkle to my life!

CONTENTS

ACKNOWLEDGMENTS

I am so thankful to God for His incredible favor in my life, enabling me to accomplish His kingdom purpose through His blessings. He has provided the inspiration, perseverence, passion, and ability to write this book for my own spiritual growth, to spur others on to pursue a relationship with Jesus Christ, and most of all, for His glory.

I am very grateful for my husband, Michael, who makes life sparkle with his inspiring creativity, endless energy, devotion to God and our marriage, love for learning, deep thinking, and playful sense of humor.

I am forever grateful for my parents, Steve and Susan Nelson, who introduced me to Jesus, the Giver of all good gifts. Knowing Him as my personal Savior has provided me with the opportunity to receive and enjoy everything He has prepared for me to be able to live a radiant life.

My heart is overflowing with love and gratitude for my sister, Heidi, who has shared so much of my life with me over the years. I love that she has been a part of all of my favorite stories!

I am truly thankful for each of these beautiful women - Ashley, Barbie, Debbie, Deborah, Doyletta, Jan, Julie, Karen, Laura, Linda, Lindsey, Martha, Peggy, Priscilla, Rachelle, Rose, and Sylvia - who have blessed me with their precious friendship over the years. They were also a special part of my monthly Birthstone Breakfasts.

GROUP GUIDELINES

BE COMMITTED

Be courteous to others in the group by committing to be present and on time each week. If you cannot make all or most of the meetings, wait until your schedule allows before committing to the study.

BE PREPARED

Take time to thoroughly read through the week's lesson and answer the questions early in the week so you will have plenty of time to contemplate what God is teaching you before you meet with your group.

BE TRUSTWORTHY

Make the group a safe place built on trust and filled with grace. Commit to keep everything that is shared completely confidential and not discussed outside of the group.

BE CONTROLLED

Build one another up with the words you say. Keep a guard on your tongue by not allowing any unwholesome talk to come out of your mouth. This includes slander, gossip, criticizing, arguing, complaining, boasting, lying, filthy language, and taking God's name in vain.

BE CONSIDERATE

When sharing with the group, be considerate of how long you spend talking. It is important for everyone to have ample time to share, so be sure to limit the amount of time you spend answering questions or sharing stories.

BE UNPLUGGED

Refrain from using your cell phone during the study. It is not only disruptive, but also distracts others in the group from being able to focus on all that God is teaching them.

BE PRAYERFUL

Share personal prayer requests and praises with each other. Then, spend some time in prayer during the week for those in your group, lifting up their specific needs to the Lord. Be sure to share how God is answering prayer.

I promise to follow each of these group guidelines to the best of my ability.

Signed: _____ Date: _____

PREFACE

I had just finished polishing a classic vintage rhinestone pin after transforming it into a stunning ring. I tried it on my finger knowing I might not ever want to take it off again. Oh, how it sparkled!

Over a decade ago, repurposing vintage costume jewelry started out as simply a fun hobby for me. Hunting for beautiful, old pieces with history and lots of sparkle became a part of every road trip with my husband, Michael, or any weekend that included an antique show in the area. It soon turned into something more serious which has included researching, speaking, blogging, and selling the pieces I had repurposed that took me back in time.

I mainly collect clip earrings, brooches, and pins from the 1940s and '50s, also known as the Golden Era. This era signified a time of both peace and prosperity. The new middle class wanted to wear jewelry that was beautiful and glamorous but also affordable as they were emerging from a time of war and extra spending money was quite limited.

Most of the pieces I've collected over the years had been designed with brilliant rhinestones in the setting. I am drawn to them because they have the most sparkle. It was later I discovered that the reason rhinestones were used during that period of time was to mimic the look of gemstones.

I really enjoy repurposing these pieces into something new and modern for today. Many of my vintage clip earrings and pins are transformed into sparkly, bold rings. Large brooches are converted into the stunning centerpieces on leather cuffs for the wrist or they become the eye-catching dazzle at the end of a long, vintage chain necklace.

As the variety of rhinestone colors grew in my collection of vintage costume jewelry, I became curious about the actual gemstones they represented.

A NEW VENTURE IN JEWELRY DESIGN

For me to be able to see and touch authentic gemstones, I needed to take a trip to one of our local bead stores and have a look around.

So that's exactly what I did.

When I walked in, I was speechless! I had never been to a bead store quite like this. It was enormous. Rows and rows of beautiful gemstone beads lined the walls, perfectly organized according to color. Most were labeled, so I was able to discover what each of the gemstones looked like in a cut and polished fashion. I now understood why jewelry designers imitated these gorgeous, natural stones!

That trip to the bead store began my next venture into jewelry design as it sparked my imagination to create trendy gemstone bracelets, necklaces, and earrings in a variety of fashionable styles and colors.

I have enjoyed selling these contemporary pieces along with my repurposed vintage jewelry at speaking engagements, jewelry shows, charming boutiques, on my website, and through social media. But I must say, I have had the most fun giving them as birthday gifts to my girlfriends, seeing their faces light up when they open my newest gemstone creation.

FOR THE LOVE OF BIRTHDAYS

I admit, I am a birthday fanatic. To me, it's a great excuse to be able to celebrate close friends in a wonderful way. My favorite way of celebrating is to treat a girlfriend to a lovely meal, giving her my time to let her know how important she is to me. There is something about having undistracted, face-to-face time that makes the celebration extra special.

Birthdays are very important. They signify the day that you were born into this world, beautifully and artistically made by the Creator of the entire universe! At the moment of conception, the Master Artist breathed life into you and began knitting you together with love in your mother's womb. Birthdays are incredibly special and should definitely be celebrated in a big way!

As much as I love birthdays, I figured I should take some time to become educated about the birthstones that represent each month of the year.

During my research, I discovered that the American National Association of Jewelers, now known as Jewelers of America, made a decision to standardize birthstones in 1912. They officially adopted a list which was updated in 1952 by The Jewelry Industry Council of America.

The following birthstone list is currently used today (updated in 2019) to identify the particular gemstones associated with each month:

- January– Garnet
- February– Amethyst
- March– Aquamarine, Bloodstone
- April– Diamond
- May– Emerald
- June– Pearl, Moonstone, Alexandrite
- July– Ruby
- August– Peridot, Spinel
- September– Sapphire
- October– Opal, Tourmaline
- November– Topaz, Citrine
- December– Turquoise, Zircon, Tanzanite

KINGDOM SPARKLE

For the past few years, I have enjoyed writing a blog called *Spiritual Sparkle*, connecting the jewelry I design to the sparkle God offers us within the promises found in His Word. I gave some deep thought into how I might be able to relate that sparkle in some way to each birthstone.

As I began to write, I realized God has some incredibly amazing gifts in store for us when we accept His Son, Jesus Christ, as our Savior. These gifts sparkle brighter than anything you could ever find in this world. It is not like any other kind of sparkle. This is *kingdom* sparkle, lasting through eternity!

These twelve gifts include friendship, royalty, grace, clarity, rest, purity, wisdom, intimacy, victory, uniqueness, joy, and stability. Instead of having to wait until we are with Him in eternity to receive these gifts, He offers them to us to enjoy right now so we can live radiant lives, beautifully reflecting His glory.

Just as the rhinestones in the vintage costume jewelry are used to resemble the look of gemstones, we are to resemble Christ, shining brightly for Him. And He graciously gives us everything we need to be able to accomplish that purpose.

AN ABUNDANT LIFE IS A RADIANT LIFE

We are all created to enjoy a personal, intimate relationship with God. There is nothing else that will ultimately satisfy our souls and bring us complete fulfillment. He provides everything we need spiritually to give us an abundant life to the fullest!

In John 10:10b (ESV) Jesus said:

I came that they may have life and have it abundantly.

The definition of *abundant* includes "richly supplied; plentiful; overflowing; more than sufficient." God created us so we would not be satisfied with anything less than abundance. He made us to want more.

The abundant life that Jesus is talking about is not a result of your external circumstances that will one day vanish (nice house, new car, job success) but rather, the result of who you are on the inside which is eternal. The more you desire God, the more abundant your life will be.

His promise is to give you an abundance of everything that makes you more like Him so the brightness of your light will be able to help others find their way out of the darkness and into complete fulfillment through a personal relationship with Jesus Christ, the Light of the world. An abundant life is a radiant life!

MY BIRTHSTONE BREAKFASTS

As I completed one *Spiritual Sparkle* birthstone blog post after another, I longed to share them with others. God knew my heart and that I wanted to use our home in some way for His glory which I had prayed about just a few months earlier. It wasn't long before He gave me the wonderful idea to host a Birthstone Breakfast each month with several of my girlfriends.

I hosted my first in January. As we all enjoyed drinking coffee and eating the variety of healthy breakfast bites I had prepared, I gave them time to visit and get to know each other. With an average of around 15 women who came regularly or had come for the first time, it was a great way for everyone to reconnect each month and to also meet new friends.

After we finished eating, I asked a question of a personal nature for each of the women to answer. Everyone was given a chance to share so we could all get to know each other a little more.

I then gave them a bit of history relating to the birthstone of the month with a prepared, biblical message describing the incredibly special gift from God associated with it. I continued to host a breakfast each month from January through December.

Once I had finished twelve blog posts and hosted the Birthstone Breakfasts for an entire year, I realized the sparkle we see in these gemstones is just a hint of the sparkle God has for us through His eternal gifts for a radiant life. And that is how this book, *Kingdom Sparkle*, came to be.

INTRODUCTION

THE PURPOSE OF THIS STUDY

There is something amazing that happens the moment we believe in Jesus Christ as our Savior. We are given the Holy Spirit, our Helper, to dwell within us so we can live a righteous, godly life. Over time, He transforms us to look more and more like Christ, radiant with His light.

We live in a pretty dark, self-serving, and sin-filled world. Things are only going to grow darker as time passes, so we must shine brighter! When your light shines, people definitely notice. With God as your light source, He gives you all you need to overcome the darkness and experience a radiant life.

"If you are filled with light, with no dark corners, then your whole life will be radiant, as though a floodlight were filling you with light."

Luke 11:36 NLT

Throughout this study, you will discover twelve gifts that will help your life sparkle brightly for Christ. These are gifts that He graciously offers you simply because you belong to Him. You will learn how to use each of them to the fullest during your time here on earth so you can be a beautiful reflection of Christ and prepared for an incredible eternity in His magnificent kingdom.

KEY VERSE FOR A RADIANT LIFE

At the beginning of each lesson you will find the Key Verse for a Radiant Life which I encourage you to memorize. The more of God's Word you have hidden in your heart and mind, the more you will grow spiritually. His Word has the power to transform you by changing you to be more like Him. Your attitude, behavior, and even your countenance changes the more you read His Word and commit it to memory.

When memorizing a verse, read it several times out loud, including the reference. Think through the topic of what you are memorizing and how it applies to you. Then, take some time to talk to God about it in prayer.

Break down the verse into small parts, repeating each part over and over until you can put it all together and say it accurately. After you have it memorized, write it out to deepen the impression of it in your mind. Put the verse in a place where you can see it and then review it frequently over the next few days. Repetition is vital to be able to commit it to memory.

The more verses you memorize, the more you will notice them popping into your mind whenever you need them most. That is how God speaks to you, helping you make wise decisions that honor Him for a godly life.

QUESTIONS

Throughout each lesson, you will be given several questions to answer as honestly as you can to help you relate the topic to your own life. If you are going to be meeting with a group, complete the questions for each lesson (or lessons) beforehand so you will be ready to discuss them with the others in your group.

PRAYER AND ACTION

Every lesson will conclude with a way to help you apply what you have learned through prayer and action. You can choose to use the written prayer or the blank "Journal" page to write out your own personal prayer and to also journal what you've learned through taking the action suggested. These are included to help you grow in your walk with Christ as you talk to Him in prayer and live out sharing His love with others in practical ways.

LESSON ONE

JANUARY'S BIRTHSTONE: GARNET
The Gift of Friendship

LESSON ONE

January's Birthstone: Garnet - The Gift of Friendship

KEY VERSE FOR A RADIANT LIFE

Sweet friendships refresh the soul and awaken our hearts with joy, for good friends are like the anointing oil that yields the fragrant incense of God's presence.

Proverbs 27:9 TPT

PLANTING SEEDS THAT NURTURE DEEP FRIENDSHIPS

"Would you like to meet me for coffee this week?"

I cannot tell you how much it means to me to hear those words from a friend. To be offered someone's precious time, along with the authentic desire for us to get to know each other more deeply, is one of the best gifts I could ever receive. In a hurried world of tight schedules with little or no margin, a person's time is truly a gift, especially when it results in a richer, more meaningful friendship.

Time is precious because each one of us has a set amount of it which cannot be replaced. Once it is used, you can never get it back. It's a portion of your life that is gone forever. Time is truly one of the most valuable gifts you can give to someone.

The friends you have had throughout your life helped shape you into who you are today. You learn things along the way from every friend. They tell you the truth about yourself. They inspire and encourage you to reach your goals and sharpen your mind. They keep you from feeling lonely, discouraged, and depressed. Best of all, they can help you live a longer, healthier life.

Who are some of the friends that come to mind who have helped shape you into who you are today?

JANUARY'S BIRTHSTONE

January's traditional birthstone is the rich, red garnet belonging to the isometric crystal class which produces symmetrical, cube-shaped crystals. Most garnets are found at the earth's surface, forming within the crust. Some, however, are created in volcanic eruptions deep below the earth's mantle, enduring extreme temperatures and pressures.

Although red is the most common, a variety of other colors of garnets have been found when mining in different countries including orange (Mozambique), green (Namibia), pink (Tanzania), yellow (Mali), and reddish purple (Sri Lanka). Red garnets are found in India.

The name *garnet* comes from the Latin word *garanatus* which means "seed-like." Garnets look much like the red seeds you find inside of a pomegranate. When used in making jewelry, garnets are traditionally arranged close together resembling what you see when you break open a pomegranate.

This beautiful Bohemian garnet pin from the Victorian era (late 1800s) is a perfect example. I found my treasure on an antiquing excursion in Eureka Springs, Arkansas:

HEALTH BENEFITS OF POMEGRANATE SEEDS

The juicy, tart seeds of a pomegranate are considered a "superfood" meaning they have numerous health benefits for the mind and body because they are so nutrient-dense and rich in antioxidants.

Here are three health benefits from eating these shiny, red jewels:

They decrease inflammation. The antioxidants in pomegranate seeds act as anti-inflammatory agents in the body, helping to reduce joint pain inflammation in those who suffer from arthritis.

They help prevent atherosclerosis. As an artery-cleansing food, the antioxidants remove excess fat and help to prevent hardening of the walls of the arteries.

They help your memory. The antioxidants in this superfood encourage blood to flow to the brain to assist in keeping brain function sharp.

You will never find a pomegranate with only one seed in it. Each can hold over 600 seeds! The health benefits result from eating *many* seeds, not just one.

HEALTH BENEFITS OF FRIENDSHIPS

Just as pomegranate seeds can provide amazing health benefits, planting *many* seeds that nurture a friendship will also offer an advantage to your physical and mental health.

Here are three health benefits of friendship:

Friends help you reach your health and fitness goals. Whether you're trying to lose weight, improve your diet, or give up unhealthy habits, a friend's encouragement can boost your willpower and motivation, increasing your chances of success.

Friends reduce your stress and depression. Having an active social life reduces isolation which is a huge contributing factor to depression. A good friendship is a great antidepressant! Friends also help decrease levels of the stress hormone cortisol.

Friends improve your mood. Spending time with cheerful, positive, and upbeat friends can elevate your mood and boost your whole outlook on life.

PLANT THE SEED OF EFFORT

A good friendship must always be two-sided. If you have ever had a relationship where you feel like you are the only one putting forth any effort in communicating or getting together, you know how hard it is to keep that friendship going. It usually doesn't last. The effort must come from both sides because it shows how much each of you care about investing in the friendship. Without effort, your friend will simply become just another acquaintance.

Texting a friend to let them know you are thinking of them is a nice gesture, but friendships cannot live on texts alone. It's important to take a little more time and effort to talk on the phone occasionally. How uplifting it is to hear a friend's voice on the other end! Having a conversation where you can share real emotions instead of emojis and laugh out loud together instead of simply texting "LOL" adds so much more richness to a friendship.

Make face-to-face time a priority. Meet with your friend in person for lunch or take a walk together on a pretty day. A great way to strengthen your friendship is to find an activity you would both enjoy and invite your friend to share that experience with you. How valued your friend will feel knowing you made the extra effort to find a fun activity to share together!

A few years ago, a friend of mine invited me to a fabulous chocolate festival which I will never forget. We both love chocolate, so after I happily accepted her offer she bought a ticket to the event for me and told me it was her treat. I felt so special! She made an effort to spend time with me and I knew, without a doubt, that she truly valued our friendship.

If you have anyone in your life who makes an effort to get together with you, be sure to be responsive and consider yourself very blessed! If you ignore their invitation or put off getting together with your friend who has offered their valuable time to you, they may quit asking. So it is important to be courteous and respond graciously. If you cannot get together at that time, make the effort to reach out to them to put another date on the calendar that works for both of you. This conveys the message that you sincerely value your friendship.

On that same note, if you ask a friend to set aside time for you to get together, be sure to do everything in your power to keep that time reserved for them. It is never good to make plans with someone only to break them again and again. Be a loyal friend by keeping your commitment to them.

Make the effort to show up on time as well which is communicating that you are a person of your word, the foundation of reliability. This is important because relationships are built on trust.

What do you do to put forth effort into maintaining your friendships?

PLANT THE SEED OF OPENNESS

Be willing to share your life with a trusted friend. What are you passionate about or what are some of the difficulties you are going through right now where you could use encouragement? If you only talk about surface subjects like the weather, sports, or the latest fashions, your friendship will never progress toward intimacy. Share from the heart. And when your friend opens up and shares deeply with you, be sure to be fully present and a good listener.

When you are enjoying face-to-face time with a friend, how present are you? There are so many distractions going on around us that it is very easy to pay attention to everything *but* the person sitting across from us.

One of the worst distractions can be the cell phone. I say this because I have experienced that uncomfortable feeling of sitting there, eating a meal in silence for several minutes (which seemed like an eternity) while my friend across from me is texting madly about something much more important than our conversation.

What a statement it would make about how much you value your friend if you put your phone away during the short time you have while sharing that special face-to-face time together! It also says, "I respect your time which is the most valuable gift you could give me and I want to be fully present for you."

To be "fully present" means to immerse yourself in the moment, completely focused on your friend sitting there in front of you and all they are sharing with you. You are engaged in the conversation, listening intently without interruption or thinking about what you are going to say next. You ask relevant questions and allow your friend to share equally. You give good eye contact so they know you are really listening. These actions don't come easy for most people and definitely take practice!

They are important actions to master, however, when you think about how it feels to share your feelings with someone only to realize their mind (and eyes) are elsewhere. It seems like a waste of words and your valuable time, not to mention how hurtful it may feel to you. There is so much to be gained from being fully present and actively engaged…like keeping a good friend!

Do you find it easy or difficult to be open with a trusted friend, sharing beyond the surface? _____ What makes it easy or difficult for you to share from your heart?

PLANT THE SEED OF DEPENDABILITY

Be the kind of friend someone can count on to be there for them. If you are not dependable, your friendship will never last. A dependable friend is trustworthy, on time, and keeps their promises, doing exactly what they say they will do.

Do you consider yourself to be a dependable kind of friend? Why or why not?

One who has unreliable friends soon comes to ruin, but there is a friend who sticks closer than a brother.

Proverbs 18:24

Other words for *unreliable* include *undependable, untrustworthy, fickle,* and *fair-weather.*

Have you ever had a friend who was unreliable?_____ If so, how did it affect your friendship?

Dependable friendships require commitment. It's easy to be a friend to someone when they are healthy, happy, and fun to be around. But the test of a true friendship is when you help to bear their burdens with them, being uplifting and supporting when they are going through the tough stuff. Be the kind of friend you would want to have when you are going through a difficult time.

Perhaps your friend has an important medical test coming up. Let her know you are praying for her and then follow up after the test to find out the results. My friends have always been extremely grateful when I let them know I am lifting them up in prayer and take the extra effort to follow up with a phone call to them after their doctor visits.

When you have a good friend, you can enjoy each other's company and conversation. You are there to bear each other's burdens and lovingly serve, sharpen, encourage, strengthen, and comfort one another.

Friendships are truly vital for good health! Be sure to plant plenty of seeds to nurture those valuable friendships.

CULTIVATE CONNECTIONS

There are more Americans living alone and aging alone now than ever before. With a greater number of people networking online rather than in person, there are fewer face-to-face interactions as well. Without them, our intimate connections and social bonds begin to atrophy. Even for those with hundreds of "friends" on Facebook, there is no substitute for building human relationships the old-fashioned way…in person.

American philosopher and psychologist William James wisely stated this over a century ago:

"Human beings are born into this little span of life of which the best thing is its friendships and intimacies…and yet they leave their friendships and intimacies with no cultivation, to grow as they will by the roadside, expecting them to "keep" by force of mere inertia."

Cultivation requires effort and time, both of which many people are not willing to give. Without meaningful friendships and intimacy with others, however, loneliness can set in. When left untreated, it can actually have serious medical consequences. Studies have linked loneliness and social isolation to depression, heart disease, cancer, diabetes, and suicide.

How often do you find yourself feeling lonely?

_____ often

_____ sometimes

_____ rarely

BE OPEN TO NEW FRIENDS

It's not always easy to find people that you really enjoy being around and with whom you want to spend your time. That's one reason it feels so much easier to stay in your tight circle of friendships that are comfortable to you. You may not even have much of a desire to be open to new relationships.

Friendships change and grow just as we do. A few stay for a lifetime but most come and go, so it's good to be open to new friends who come into your life. You never know the blessings that are in store for you when you give and receive through friendship.

There are many different ways new friendships can start. If you don't have any close friends, ask God to show you someone to whom you can reach out who needs a friend like you. He knows who might be praying that exact same prayer. It's no problem for Him to figure out how to connect the two of you.

You don't have to wait for others to invite you to connect. Be friendly and take the initiative toward a new friendship by inviting someone to get together with you. Over time, the more you invest in your friend and they in you, the more your friendship will grow.

Last year, a kindhearted caretaker frequently brought her elderly client to the exercise classes I taught for a senior community. We had many conversations before and after class, often about the goodness of God in our lives. I loved her heart for God and wanted to get to know her more, so I invited her to come to one of my breakfasts that I continued to host after the year of my Birthstone Breakfasts. To my surprise, she said she would love to come!

Our friendship grew from there, sharing praises and prayer requests with each other, texting words of encouragement, and celebrating our birthdays together. I am so glad I was open to a new friend and had made the effort to connect more deeply with her.

Has God ever put someone on your heart to reach out to and get to know? _____ If so, how did you react to His prompting?

BUILD THE BONDS OF CLOSE CONNECTION

We have all been born with a natural desire for personal engagement with someone in whom we can confide and have a meaningful, heartfelt relationship. It's how God created us.

If your relationships seem shallow, you may begin to experience feelings of loneliness. You cannot easily share your heart on a deeper level with someone you don't know very well. Loneliness can be a good wake-up call that you need to be building stronger bonds with others.

To help make your friendships more meaningful, here are a few ways you can strengthen the bonds between you and others with whom you enjoy spending time...

RESPOND

Think about ways you can celebrate a friend. Is their birthday coming up? Did they recently land a new job or get promoted? Complete a major project? Have a baby or adopt a child? Finish graduate school? Buy a new house?

Knowing what is happening in someone's life allows you to be able to be intentional with your connection. When you celebrate them, you are expressing gratitude for the blessing their friendship has brought to you.

Do more than just send them a card to congratulate them. Ask to meet up so you can help them celebrate properly! Be enthusiastic about their good news and ask to hear about all the details. Responding to others in a positive way makes them feel more understood and cared for which definitely strengthens the bond between you and your friend.

I took a girlfriend out to celebrate her new job after many months of praying for her. When I received a card in the mail from her soon afterward, I understood just how much it means to celebrate victories with others and to let them know you are rejoicing with them. She wrote:

Thank you for wanting to celebrate with me. I will always remember that night.

REMINISCE

It may have been a long time since you've seen one of your friends. Sometimes, it just takes a little reminiscing of fun times from the past to strengthen the bond again. Sharing and savoring memories brings people closer together. When you meet, perhaps you can take along a photo of a memory and enjoy recollecting the details and memorable moments during the time you spent together.

REVEAL

Often, the strongest adhesive between two people is the trust that develops after sharing fears, faults, and insecurities. Yes, it makes you vulnerable and may even push you out of your comfort zone a bit, but it's worth it for the depth and closeness you will experience in your relationship. Of course, it must go both ways. Your friend needs to be able to share their heart with you as well for that strong bond to occur.

THE STRONGEST ADHESIVE

When I first began repurposing vintage costume jewelry into sparkly rings several years ago, I was using an adhesive to bond the vintage piece to a ring base.

Unfortunately, it was not nearly as strong as I expected. As a result, many of my rings ended up in two pieces as they detached from their bases over time.

I did a little research to find out the best way to bond them permanently together and thankfully, figured out the problem. I needed to be using a two-part epoxy adhesive.

Two-part epoxy is made up of a resin and a hardener. Chemical bonds that form between the resin and the hardener are what control the strength of the epoxy. Together, they are very stable and can withstand almost any kind of resistance.

The bond that forms between two people must also be ultra strong or the relationship will simply fall apart with time. The strongest adhesive between two people is when both are living for Jesus Christ. He wants us to create meaningful relationships. Those with strong bonds take time and effort with consistent connection.

Your relationship with God is the same way. When you make the time each day to talk with Him in prayer and read His Word, you are strengthening the bond between you and God. You are getting to know Him more intimately, learning to trust Him, and experiencing His deep love for you as you share your heart with Him. When you are completely connected to Him, you can feel His presence and no longer have to suffer from loneliness.

Draw near to God and he will draw near to you.

James 4:8a ESV

How connected do you feel to God right now?

THE KOINONIA CONNECTION

God knows the importance of relationships and created us with a natural desire for fellowship because He never intended for us to live this life all alone. The word that best describes ideal fellowship and unity among those who follow Christ is the Greek word *koinonia*.

Koinonia occurs 20 times throughout the Bible. Its essential meanings include "community, communion, joint participation, sharing, and intimacy."

The first place koinonia is found in the Bible is in Acts:

They were continually devoting themselves to the apostles' teaching and to fellowship, to the breaking of bread and to prayer.

Acts 2:42 NASB

Koinonia is a necessary part of being a follower of Christ. It is based on the koinonia we have with Him. Believers are to be united in purpose, loving each other, lifting one another up in prayer, and serving together.

The Apostle Paul stressed the importance of spiritual unity when he wrote to the believers at Philippi:

Therefore if you have any encouragement from being united with Christ, if any comfort from his love, if any common sharing in the Spirit, if any tenderness and compassion, then make my joy complete by being like-minded, having the same love, being one in spirit and of one mind.

Philippians 2:1-2

Those with whom you spend the most time will influence you. If you are a follower of Christ, your closest friends should encourage you toward spiritual growth, sharing your enthusiasm for following Jesus.

Who are some of the friends in your life with whom you have a koinonia connection?

ENCOURAGE ONE ANOTHER

Another important part of koinonia is encouraging each other in your walk with Christ. At times, you may feel like you are constantly encouraging others without getting much encouragement in return. But know that when you are doing God's will by filling others up with His uplifting truths and a listening ear, He will make sure you are also filled up in the ways He knows will encourage you most. I have personally experienced this many times in my own life with an encouraging phone call, text, or thoughtful card I received in the mail just when I really needed it.

Spending some time to express to your friend how much you appreciate them goes a long way. If they have been kind or thoughtful toward you, be sure to thank them! Those two little words "thank you" can mean so much to a person when they are acknowledged for their efforts.

Show your appreciation by being generous with your words – in the moment. If there is something you admire about your friend, let them know right then and there. It is such a boost to the heart, mind, and spirit to hear affirming words.

PRECIOUS TREASURES

Good friends are precious treasures. They show us how to forgive, make conversation, be ourselves, laugh, share our hearts, our failures, and our successes. They ease feelings of loneliness and help us calm down when we are stressed out by putting things in perspective. They listen, support, and encourage us. They fill us with joy. Good friends are vital to our well-being and refresh our soul!

Sweet friendships refresh the soul and awaken our hearts with joy, for good friends are like the anointing oil that yields the fragrant incense of God's presence.

Proverbs 27:9 TPT

Jesus Christ is the ultimate example of our faithful friend. He gave His life so the friendship between us would never have to end. Because of His sacrifice, He made a way for our sins to be forgiven so we could be with Him for eternity.

Greater love has no one than this: to lay down one's life for one's friends.

John 15:13

Because of Christ's great love for us, we are empowered to share His love with others for deep connection and fellowship so we can enjoy the beautiful gift of friendship for a radiant life.

Dear Heavenly Father,

Thank You for the gift of friendship. Please give me a heart that is open to new friends so I can share Your love with them. I pray that I would cultivate the friendships You have given me by planting seeds of effort, openness, and dependability. I ask that You would bring people into my life with whom I can experience koinonia for the best fellowship and unity through You. Thank You for being my faithful friend and for the unbreakable bond between us so I never have to feel lonely.

In Jesus' name,

Amen

TAKE ACTION

Invite a friend this week to spend some face-to-face time with you, perhaps on a walk or over a cup of coffee where you can listen intently to each other for a richer, more meaningful relationship.

Find a friend in your life who has had a recent achievement or birthday and celebrate with them! Be an encouragement to them through your efforts and watch how God encourages you in return. Take some time to journal how you have been encouraged through friendship.

LESSON TWO

FEBRUARY'S BIRTHSTONE: AMETHYST
The Gift of Royalty

LESSON TWO

February's Birthstone: Amethyst - The Gift of Royalty

KEY VERSE FOR A RADIANT LIFE

For he has rescued us from the kingdom of darkness and transferred us into the Kingdom of his dear Son, who purchased our freedom and forgave our sins.

Colossians 1:13-14 NLT

LIVE LIKE A ROYAL

It all began as a small boutique. In 1901, Emanuel Cohn and Carl Rosenberger partnered to establish a costume jewelry company on Broadway in New York City. They used the first two letters of each of their last names to form the name Coro.

Despite the onset of the Great Depression, Coro opened a factory in 1929 to manufacture their jewelry in Providence, Rhode Island, one of the main hubs for jewelry production in the U.S. since the 18th century.

Coro grew rapidly with several retail stores, showrooms, and factories opening throughout the U.S., Canada, and England. It wasn't long before they became the world's largest costume jewelry manufacturer.

One of my most favorite Coro pieces found during a treasure hunt for vintage costume jewelry is a sparkly rhinestone pin with tiny pearls from the 1950s in a magnificent shade of purple:

FEBRUARY'S BIRTHSTONE

This Coro pin reminds me of February's traditional birthstone which is the beautiful gemstone amethyst, a violet variety of the mineral quartz which is one of the most common minerals on earth. Its hue of purple ranges from pale lilac to deep violet, attributed to the amount of iron and manganese it contains.

Amethyst is a common gemstone found on every continent. Huge deposits of it in South America and Africa provide enough to keep the price of amethyst low. Brazil is the largest producer yielding two to three thousand tons each year followed by Zambia, producing around one thousand tons annually.

THE COLOR PURPLE

The color purple has been associated with royalty for centuries. In literary works, purple often symbolizes wealth, power, and status. Far back in history, purple's elite status came from the rarity and high cost of the dye to produce it. It was so expensive that only rulers could afford it. Queen Elizabeth I, who reigned from 1558 to 1603, forbade anyone except close members of the royal family to wear it.

Fabric traders would acquire the dye from a small mollusk found only in the Tyre region of the Mediterranean Sea, now modern-day Lebanon. More than 9,000 mollusks were necessary to create just one gram of Tyrian purple! It soon became associated with the royal classes of Rome, Egypt, and Persia.

Purple was worn by royalty during biblical times as well. For example, Judges 8:26 describes the plunder after Gideon captured and killed Zebah and Zalmunna, the two kings of Midian:

The weight of the gold rings he asked for came to seventeen hundred shekels, not counting the ornaments, the pendants and the purple garments worn by the kings of Midian or the chains that were on their camels' necks.

ADOPTED INTO ROYALTY

Did you know that the moment you ask Jesus Christ to come into your life to be your Savior you instantly become royalty? You are adopted as a child of the King, welcomed into the royal family of God!

Jesus was asked a question about royalty by Pilate just before His crucifixion:

Therefore Pilate said to Him, "So you are a king?" Jesus answered, "You say correctly that I am a king. For this I have been born, and for this I have come into the world, to testify to the truth. Everyone who is of the truth hears My voice."

John 18:37 NASB

Jesus is the King of Truth. His truths are written in His Word that He has given to you so He can speak directly to your heart. If you have given Him your heart, you will hear and recognize His voice as your Father, the King, because you are His child.

Years ago, I had a dear friend who could not have any children of her own. Because of this heartache, she and her husband made the decision to adopt two little girls from two separate families. The moment they were adopted as their own, they were given a new last name – the same name as their adoptive parents. They belonged to them.

One of the girls was quite a handful and had some behavioral issues that made parenting quite difficult, to say the least. The other was much more easy-going and very compliant – a parent's dream child! But the amount of love they had for each of their daughters was equal. There was nothing either of them could do, or not do, to make their parents love them less.

When you receive Jesus Christ as your Savior, He adopts you as His child. And He loves you just how you are. There is nothing you could do, or not do, to make Him love you less. Yes, you are a sinner and maybe you have even done some horrible, unspeakable things in your life that seem unforgivable, yet He still sees you as righteous and without fault. Isn't that incredible?

Even before he made the world, God loved us and chose us in Christ to be holy and without fault in his eyes. God decided in advance to adopt us into his own family by bringing us to himself through Jesus Christ.

Ephesians 1:4-5a NLT

According to His Word, how does God see you?

God adopts us because He wants to know us intimately, like family. When you are His child, you belong to Him. He sees right past all of your flaws and He loves you unconditionally.

See how very much our Father loves us, for he calls us his children, and that is what we are! But the people who belong to this world don't recognize that we are God's children because they don't know him.

1 John 3:1 NLT

IMMEASURABLE VALUE

In our society, the value of something is often determined by the maximum amount someone will pay for it.

Nine years ago, my precious little Pomeranian, Emma, was auctioned off with several other Poms after the filthy, run-down puppy mill where she lived had been shut down. A Pomeranian rescue group from Dallas happened to be there, along with other puppy mill breeders.

When it was time for Emma to be sold, the price for her kept rising. Although she was underweight, matted, and dirty from living in a cage for most of her life, her beauty was still very noticeable.

It then became a competition between the rescuers getting her out of there into a loving home and the breeders taking her with them to use her to birth more puppies, possibly going back into the exact same kind of horrific living conditions. This rescue group was determined to save her.

Their determination paid off, bidding the highest amount anyone at the auction was willing to pay. This allowed them to take Emma home with them that day, along with 21 other very privileged Poms. Once she was ready for adoption, I paid a price for her and she belonged to me from that day on.

In order for you to be adopted, Jesus paid the very highest price for you. He shed His own blood, giving His life for you even though you were damaged and dirty. Why? Because, as your Creator, He could look right past all of the filth of your sin and shame and see your beauty. He did not want you to be stuck in hopelessness, dead in your sins. He wanted you to have freedom through Him and a new life!

Because of Jesus, you have immeasurable value.

Your Father, the King, loves you no matter who you are or what you've done and *nothing* can ever separate you from His love.

In the Apostle Paul's letter to the Romans, he writes:

And I am convinced that nothing can ever separate us from God's love. Neither death nor life, neither angels nor demons, neither our fears for today nor our worries about tomorrow—not even the powers of hell can separate us from God's love. No power in the sky above or in the earth below—indeed, nothing in all creation will ever be able to separate us from the love of God that is revealed in Christ Jesus our Lord.

Romans 8:38-39 NLT

Have you ever questioned whether you are worthy of God's love for you? _____ If so, what has caused you to think you might be unworthy of His love?

THE BENEFITS OF BEING A ROYAL

Being a part of a royal family includes numerous benefits…

Royalty always has protection wherever they go. As a child of the King, you have angels constantly watching over you and protecting you.

For he will order his angels to protect you wherever you go.

Psalm 91:11 NLT

Royalty never has to worry about their needs being met. As a child of the King, His riches provide everything you need.

And my God will supply all your needs according to His riches in glory in Christ Jesus.

Philippians 4:19 NASB

Royalty dresses only in the finest garments. As a child of the King, you are given the garments of salvation and a robe of righteousness paid for by Jesus' priceless, shed blood so you may live with Him, free from sin in His kingdom forever.

I will greatly rejoice in the LORD; my soul shall exult in my God, for he has clothed me with the garments of salvation; he has covered me with the robe of righteousness, as a bridegroom decks himself like a priest with a beautiful headdress, and as a bride adorns herself with her jewels.

Isaiah 61:10 ESV

Royalty is surrounded by beauty. As a child of the King, you will be surrounded by incredible beauty, splendor, and magnificence in your new Home in heaven. One of the foundations of the wall of the city just so happens to be amethyst, a royal gemstone!

The foundations of the wall of the city were adorned with every kind of jewel. The first was jasper, the second sapphire, the third agate, the fourth emerald, the fifth onyx, the sixth carnelian, the seventh chrysolite, the eighth beryl, the ninth topaz, the tenth chrysoprase, the eleventh jacinth, the twelfth amethyst. And the twelve gates were twelve pearls, each of the gates made of a single pearl, and the street of the city was pure gold, like transparent glass.

Revelation 21:19-21 ESV

Royalty wears a beautiful crown. The Greek word *crown* means "a badge of royalty." As a child of the King, you will receive the crown of life, given to those who love Him.

Happy is the man who doesn't give in and do wrong when he is tempted, for afterwards he will get as his reward the crown of life that God has promised those who love him.

James 1:12 TLB

If you ever question being worthy of God's love for you, just remember who you are. You are a child of the King, a part of the royal family of God! Nothing can ever separate you from His love. He has rescued you out of the kingdom of darkness so you may forever be with Him in His Kingdom of light!

May you be filled with joy, always thanking the Father. He has enabled you to share in the inheritance that belongs to his people, who live in the light. For he has rescued us from the kingdom of darkness and transferred us into the Kingdom of his dear Son, who purchased our freedom and forgave our sins.

Colossians 1:11(b)-14 NLT

What are five benefits of being a royal when you are adopted into God's family?

A ROYAL CALLING

At the beginning of 2018, I thoughtfully chose my new word for the new year. It's something I like to do every time January rolls around. I picked a word that I believed would challenge my faith and trust in God. A word that would bring promise to me no matter how my "big dream" turned out. This was a dream I had resolved to work hard to accomplish during the next 12 months.

So, my word I chose for the year was BEYOND, based on Ephesians 3:20 (TLB):

Now glory be to God, who by his mighty power at work within us is able to do far more than we would ever dare to ask or even dream of—infinitely beyond our highest prayers, desires, thoughts, or hopes.

MY BIG DREAM

My idea of BEYOND is using my speaking and writing gifts in a really big way. For a very long time, I have envisioned my calendar completely booked up with speaking engagements for women's groups in churches all across the Dallas Metroplex on the topic of my first book I wrote titled, *Beauty in a Life Repurposed.* For me, that would be a big dream come true.

With all of the effort, focus, and time I was giving toward trying to make my dream become a reality (numerous phone calls, emails, and hours of preparation), I figured certainly God must be right on board with this, too.

Here I am pursuing something that uses the gifts He gave me and it is a way for me to share God's encouraging message to many women at one time about how He can repurpose us through our trials so we can shine brightly and beautifully once again. Something everyone needs to hear, right?

THE EXCHANGE

Funny how our dreams, no matter how good they seem, are not always what God intends for us. There is one particular verse that often pops into my mind whenever I start to think about how my big dream is NOT happening as I planned:

"For my thoughts are not your thoughts, neither are your ways my ways," declares the LORD. "As the heavens are higher than the earth, so are my ways higher than your ways and my thoughts than your thoughts."

Isaiah 55:8-9

Have you ever realized that your big dream was not a part of God's plan for you? _____ How did you react?

When our big dream is not a part of God's plan for us, it can be very stressful, creating anxiety within us when it constantly feels like a struggle to make it happen. When we give our dream to God, however, and allow Him to exchange it for His plan for our lives, we experience perfect peace. He is the Master at being able to make anything within His plan to transpire without the added stress.

What dream of yours do you struggle to let go, knowing it may not be a part of God's plan for you?

Although it felt like I was over-striving, I still had a very hard time giving my dream to God. It felt like giving up. Hard to do when you spend hours of your life trying to make something happen. And then one day, it just hit me...

A BEAUTIFUL REMINDER

As a collector of vintage costume jewelry, I am always on the hunt for good quality, unique pieces to repurpose. I had recently found an exceptionally beautiful jeweled rhinestone crown pin from the 1940s, owned by an antique collector. When I saw this colorful crown with so much sparkle, it immediately reminded me of who I am...a daughter of the King!

As a daughter of the King, I do not need to over-strive for anything that is within His will and perfect plan for my life. Because He is the King, everything is within His power and ability. If He wants it to happen, it will happen! All I am asked to do is acknowledge He is my King and let Him lead.

THE KING IS YOUR CREATOR

Your Father, the King, knows everything about you because He made you. He knows what makes you tick, what brings you joy, and has a perfect plan for your life because He deeply loves you and desires for you to be fulfilled with purpose. It is a plan which He has had in mind for you before He even began forming you in your mother's womb!

Your eyes have seen my unformed substance; and in Your book were all written the days that were ordained for me, when as yet there was not one of them.

Psalm 139:16 NASB

As a child of the King, you never have to question the doors He opens and closes for you because He knows which will lead you to follow His perfectly designed plan for your life. You can pull hard on the closed doors, creating stress and anxiety because they seem impossible to open, or you can walk effortlessly through the doors that He is holding wide open for you.

His purpose for your life is not about your big dream. It is a royal calling!

THE KING IS ALL-KNOWING

Your Father, the King, knows your past, present, and future. He knows how you can best bring glory to Him with your gifts because of your past experiences, the people He is presently putting on your path to serve, and those who will come into your life in the future. He is all-knowing.

God promises that His plans for you give you a future where you will flourish and thrive. You can look forward to God's destiny for your life with hope!

"For I know the plans I have for you," declares the LORD "plans to prosper you and not to harm you, plans to give you hope and a future."

Jeremiah 29:11

As a child of the King, He wants you to be able to rest in Him, free from stress to do exactly what He has planned for you, using your gifts for His glory. He certainly does not want you on an exhausting journey filled with anxiety while pursuing a self-serving dream to bring yourself glory.

His focus for you is always going to be on how others can be drawn toward His love through your submission and obedience to Him. And in return, you will experience complete fulfillment.

THE KING IS ALL-POWERFUL

Your Father, the King, has the power to do anything. If you are allowing Him to guide you down the path He has set out for you, there are no obstacles that can get in His way.

His plan and the steps He asks you to take toward that plan may seem impossible to you but if that is what He wants for your life, there is no need to ever worry about anything blocking it! He is all-powerful.

Great is our Lord, and abundant in power; his understanding is beyond measure.

Psalm 147:5 ESV

As a child of the King, it is important to fully trust Him. It took me a long time to finally loosen the grip on my big dream, but I am finally experiencing peace from having the freedom to let Him lead me as I am trusting Him and embracing His will for my life.

OPEN DOORS

Each day, I see a little more of His plan revealed as doors are slowly beginning to open. No, not the doors of numerous churches opening for me to speak about God's message of repurposing. Not right now, anyway. These are the doors of reconnecting with both old and new friends that are swinging wide open for me to spend quality time, deeply connecting one-on-one.

Perhaps He knows I will have a greater impact in this world if I can use my gifts connecting with one person at a time rather than speaking to large groups. Whatever the reason for these particular doors opening and not the others, the striving is far behind me.

I can now experience peace and feel like I have a true purpose, knowing I am making a difference in others' lives as I am available to listen and encourage those who are in need of knowing they are deeply loved by their Father, the King. It is my royal calling.

A man's mind plans his way, but the LORD directs his steps.
Proverbs 16:9 NASB

What doors do you see opening for you right now that may be leading you toward your royal calling?

A CHALLENGE FOR MY FAITH AND TRUST

My word, BEYOND, has definitely challenged my faith and trust in God. By finally giving my big dream to Him in exchange for His perfect plan, I am trusting my Creator who knows me best.

I am no longer leaning on my own understanding of things because I realize He is the One who is all-knowing. And I have submitted my imperfect ways of doing things to His perfect ways because He is all-powerful and has the ability to make my paths straight if I simply obey Him.

Trust in the LORD with all your heart and lean not on your own understanding; in all your ways submit to him, and he will make your paths straight.

Proverbs 3:5-6

What three acts of obedience does God ask of you for your paths to be straight?

You are a child of the King who loves you deeply, knows you intimately, and wants the very best for your life so you can quit striving and rest in Him.

If you have faith to believe His plan is infinitely better than your big dream and trust Him enough to give it to Him, He will provide you with His perfect plan, His perfect peace, and His perfect purpose for your life... BEYOND what you could ever dare to ask or even dream!

THE GIFT OF ROYALTY FOR A RADIANT LIFE

When we are adopted as a child of the King, we are rescued from the kingdom of darkness, never to be separated from God's love. With the gift of royalty, our Father is able to do far more than we could ever dare to ask or even dream for a radiant life.

Dear Heavenly Father,

Thank You for the gift of royalty. I am so grateful You paid the highest price for me with Your life so I could be adopted as Your child and live with You forever in Your kingdom. Thank You for giving me immeasurable value and for the assurance that nothing can ever separate me from Your love. I want to fully trust You as my Father, the King. I submit my will and my big dream to You so You can lead me to my royal calling for Your glory.

In Jesus' name,

Amen

TAKE ACTION

Write about your big dream you've been working hard to accomplish. Then, take some time to submit your plans to God and allow Him to lead you, even if the path ahead looks completely different from what you envision. Remember, His ways and thoughts are higher than yours!

Journal what He begins to show you about your royal calling. In time, He will provide you with the details of His perfect plan to accomplish all He wants to do through you for His glory.

LESSON THREE

MARCH'S BIRTHSTONE: AQUAMARINE
The Gift of Grace

LESSON THREE

March's Birthstone: Aquamarine - The Gift of Grace

KEY VERSE FOR A RADIANT LIFE

Let your conversation be always full of grace, seasoned with salt, so that you may know how to answer everyone.

Colossians 4:6

SEASON WITH GRACE AS SALT OF THE EARTH

My fun, energetic mother-in-law had come to town over the holidays for a visit. She loves shopping on Main Street of quaint little towns in Texas as much as I do. So this visit, Michael and I chose to take her to the historic square in downtown McKinney.

They have darling boutiques, charming cafes, and even a few antique shops. We spent the day looking for unique finds and, as always, discovering a few things we could never live without.

On our way back to the car, we spotted one final shop to browse – an antique store filled with my favorite kind of treasure…vintage costume jewelry. A woman greeted me at the door who instantly recognized me and said, "You're the girl who repurposes vintage jewelry!"

She introduced herself and said she used to be one of the antique dealers who sold vintage jewelry to me for repurposing at one of the local monthly antique shows. It had been quite a while since I had attended one of those shows, so I didn't recognize her right away. She now had her very own antique store with even more jewelry than she could have ever had at her compact booth. I couldn't wait to see it all!

She led me to each of her prized, glass cases, unlocking them one at a time so I could get a closer look at everything. One of the first pieces of jewelry I spotted was a fabulous aquamarine rhinestone ring from the 1960s era.

I thought to myself, *What are the chances it would actually fit my finger?* I tried it on and to my amazement it fit perfectly! That was one unique find definitely coming home with me.

Since then, I have picked up several other beautiful vintage pieces imitating the look of the gemstone aquamarine to repurpose into sparkly statement rings such as this lovely rhinestone beauty from the 1950s era.

MARCH'S BIRTHSTONE

Aquamarine is March's traditional birthstone whose name comes from the Latin *aqua marina* meaning "water of the sea." The pale blue color of the gemstone looks like the ocean which is how it got its name.

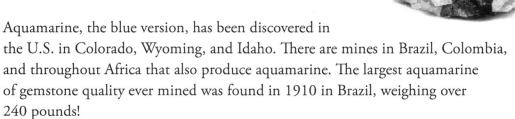

This transparent crystal is a member of the beryl family. Pure beryl is colorless, but it is often tinted by impurities (iron oxides) which add color such as green, blue, yellow, red, and white.

Aquamarine, the blue version, has been discovered in the U.S. in Colorado, Wyoming, and Idaho. There are mines in Brazil, Colombia, and throughout Africa that also produce aquamarine. The largest aquamarine of gemstone quality ever mined was found in 1910 in Brazil, weighing over 240 pounds!

SALT OF THE EARTH

Within the ocean, aqua marina, we find the salt of the earth. Approximately 3.5% of the weight of seawater comes from dissolved salts (sodium chloride). To get a better idea of how much that is, in a cubic mile of seawater the weight of the salt would be about 120 million tons.

By some estimates, if the salt in the ocean could be extracted and spread evenly over the land surface of the earth, it would form a layer greater than 500 feet thick – the height of a 40-story office building!

Did you know we are also called to be the salt of the earth?

Jesus taught his disciples saying:

"You are the salt of the earth, but if salt has lost its taste, how shall its saltiness be restored? It is no longer good for anything except to be thrown out and trampled under people's feet."

Matthew 5:13 ESV

THE PURPOSES OF SALT

Before the days of refrigeration, salt had two purposes. One was for preserving food because it absorbed water, keeping bacteria from multiplying. The other was to enhance flavor. When adding salt to foods, it reduces our perception of bitterness. As bitterness is reduced, it increases the salty taste along with our perception of the other flavors we can detect which include sweet, sour, and umami (savory).

When I was very young, I would take a walk in our big backyard toward the apple trees with my Uncle Lance whenever he came for a visit. We carried our own salt shakers with us and stood there next to each other taking a big bite out of our freshly picked green apples. But not before we sprinkled a little salt on them.

Somehow, that salt made the bitterness go away. It was a heavenly, sweet taste instead. If it was not for the cores, we would have lost count of how many apples we ate!

Both purposes, preserving food and enhancing flavor, were essential, making salt a valuable commodity. The word *salary* actually comes from an ancient word meaning "salt money."

At one time, soldiers in the Roman army were given a sum of money to buy salt for themselves. The Latin word for "salt" was *sal.* The "salt money" given to the soldiers was called *salarium* which was later used as the term for their regular salary. And that is where the English word *salary* comes from.

As followers of Christ, it is our responsibility to preserve truth and goodness in a world that is corrupt and immoral, blatantly turning away from God's laws. Like salt, our role in the world is very valuable. We are to create a positive impact on those around us, seasoning them with grace to enhance the flavor of life in this world.

Let your conversation be always full of grace, seasoned with salt, so that you may know how to answer everyone.

Colossians 4:6

When God gives us grace, He is giving us what we do not deserve. As sinners, we deserve eternal punishment but God graciously sent His Son, Jesus, to die for us so that we can be forgiven and have eternal life when we accept Him as our Savior. Showing grace to others is showing kindness to them even when we do not think they deserve it.

Have you ever demonstrated grace to someone whom you did not think was deserving? If so, how?

How did they respond?

How did it make you feel?

In order to be able to show grace (which does not come naturally to anyone), you must first have a transformation of the heart, open to letting God change you to be more like Him.

How do you know where you need change? The more you get to know God by spending time with Him reading His Word, the easier it will be to hear His voice when He is speaking to you about the areas of your life that need change. The more you know Him, the greater your desire will be to please Him.

As your heart becomes transformed, you will have a renewed way of thinking and an eagerness to show grace to others as God would want you to do. That is what being "the salt of the earth" is all about.

Just as salt loses its flavor when diluted with water, you can lose your pungency as the salt of the earth if you become watered down when conforming to the world and do not have grace.

There are several ways to exhibit grace from a transformed heart…

ATTITUDE OF HUMILITY

You must have an attitude of humility, putting others' interests before your own. We are naturally selfish and want to do what we want to do without giving a second thought about the other person. But if we are to show grace, it requires putting other people's interests first.

One way to do this is to ask meaningful questions so you can learn about who they are. Allow them to talk about themselves and then be sincerely interested in their response.

Do nothing out of selfish ambition or vain conceit. Rather, in humility value others above yourselves, not looking to your own interests but each of you to the interests of the others.

Philippians 2:3-4

A THANKFUL HEART

It costs nothing to say "thank you" but it shows others a heart of gratitude and grace. Expressing your thankfulness does not take much time but can mean so much to the person receiving it.

Being thankful reminds us that God is our Provider and the Giver of all good gifts. He never intended for you to be fully self-sufficient in this life. Having a thankful heart reminds you that every good gift you receive is from Him.

Every good and perfect gift is from above, coming down from the Father of the heavenly lights, who does not change like shifting shadows.

James 1:17

YOUR PRESENCE

If you know someone who is going through physical or emotional pain, show grace by taking time to be with them, demonstrating love simply with your presence. This can create deep healing in others in ways you may never comprehend.

Carry each other's burdens, and in this way you will fulfill the law of Christ.

Galatians 6:2

FORGIVENESS

When a person asks you for forgiveness, accept their apology with grace. They are humbling themselves, so it is important to show grace and let them know you completely forgive them. Even when they do not ask for forgiveness, give it to them anyway. Grace can help so much with repairing a relationship when you respond in a loving way.

Be kind to one another, tenderhearted, forgiving one another, as God in Christ forgave you.

Ephesians 4:32 ESV

Write about a time when you demonstrated grace through an attitude of humility, a thankful heart, your presence, or forgiveness:

Showing grace allows you to keep your testimony strong as a follower of Christ, seasoning the lives of everyone with whom God crosses your path. If you lose your testimony and become bitter in your heart, you lose your saltiness. And salt without saltiness, as Jesus said, *"is no longer good for anything except to be thrown out and trampled under people's feet."*

Becoming the salt of the earth begins with a transformed heart, a vital necessity for you to be able to be used by God for enhancing flavor in the lives of those you touch as you season them with grace – the kind of undeserved, endless, and amazing grace God gives you!

SEASON WITH GRACE THROUGH YOUR WORDS

Words. We use them every day to communicate. People have always thought women speak many more words than men. Surprisingly, the latest research has found that men and women use approximately the same number of words a day!

So often, we neglect to give much thought to our words before they come out of our mouths. We are all guilty of being careless with what we say, but we must realize words are not simply different sounds passing through our lips. Words have very real power. In fact, it was the power of God's words that spoke the world into existence!

By faith we understand that the universe was formed at God's command, so that what is seen was not made out of what is visible.

Hebrews 11:3

POWER TO DESTROY AND BUILD UP

We, too, have power in our words because we were made in God's image. It is a unique gift from God to us, unlike any other living being on this planet, to be able to communicate with words.

Our words have the power to destroy. With words, good reputations have been damaged, stable careers have been devastated, and intimate relationships have been severed. The tongue, as small as it is, can cause massive destruction.

Likewise, the tongue is a small part of the body, but it makes great boasts. Consider what a great forest is set on fire by a small spark.

James 3:5

Our words also have the power to build up. Think about how you feel when someone sincerely praises you for something that they admire in you. You probably feel a huge boost in your spirit and incredibly encouraged. A good word spoken at the right time can be life changing!

But when words have been spoken that are harsh and hurtful toward you, it has the opposite effect, tearing you down and destroying your spirit. Words are powerful!

The tongue has the power of life and death, and those who love it will eat its fruit.

Proverbs 18:21

What exactly does this verse mean?

Those who take pleasure in communicating with others will eat the fruit of their words meaning they will reap the consequences of what comes out of their mouths whether good or bad. If you are a talker like me, you probably need to put forth extra effort in thinking before you speak!

I have found Psalm 141:3 (ESV) to be a great prayer for me to say quite frequently…

Set a guard, O LORD, over my mouth; keep watch over the door of my lips!

Jesus warns strongly against careless words:

"I tell you, on the day of judgment people will give account for every careless word they speak, for by your words you will be justified, and by your words you will be condemned."

Matthew 12:36-37 ESV

Words have so much power when spoken that we are going to give an account of what we say when we stand before Jesus Christ. This may create a great deal of anxiety for you but know that although it does not exclude responsibility for your actions, He loves you no matter how much you have sinned with your words. And He forgives you so you do not have to carry around guilt and shame. He took all of that for you upon Himself when He died on the cross.

As followers of Christ, we are to be different from the rest of the world so that people will be drawn to His light in us and we can have an opportunity to share God's love for them. Use your words in a way that you can be a blessing to others by speaking with kindness.

Kind words are like honey—sweet to the soul and healthy for the body.

Proverbs 16:24 NLT

THE HEART AND MOUTH CONNECTION

Why do we say the things we say? The Bible talks about how there is a direct connection between the heart and mouth:

"For the mouth speaks out of that which fills the heart."

Matthew 12:34b NASB

Whatever is in your heart will come out of your mouth. If you are filled with anger, hostile words will come out. If you are filled with kindness, loving words will come out.

Think of your heart like a fountain and your words are the streams of water flowing out of it. If the fountain is polluted, the water will come out dirty – maybe even quite muddy! But if the fountain is clean and pure, the water will be clear and sparkling.

We all have a need for our heart to be transformed in different ways. No matter how long you have been walking with God, there are always going to be things that need to be changed inside of you. It's an on-going process of transformation while you are still here on earth.

What seems to be filling your heart right now, affecting the words that come out of your mouth?

As your relationship with God continues to grow by talking to Him in prayer and spending more time with Him in His Word, allow Him to work in you so you can be more like Him. You will slowly begin to see a change in your heart which will transfer to the way you speak. Your words will be full of blessing when your heart is full of blessing.

Words have power. Use them in a way to build one another up, not tear each other down. As you grow closer to the Lord, may your words reflect a heart that truly sparkles!

SEASON WITH GRACE THROUGH ENCOURAGEMENT

Do you ever feel like you could use a word of encouragement? The Greek word for *encourage* is *parakaleó* which means "to come alongside with strength or encouragement." Other meanings include "beseech, entreat, beg, exhort, admonish, comfort, console, instruct, and teach."

God knew we would experience feelings of discouragement and would need people to encourage us all along our journey in life. As a follower of Christ, did you know it is your duty to encourage others? It can be found 109 times in the New Testament, so it is obviously very important to God for us to obey this command!

Therefore encourage one another and build one another up, just as you are doing.

1 Thessalonians 5:11

Encouraging others is not simply offering a complimentary word of false hope. Real encouragement requires one of your most precious gifts…your time. Why? Because it requires you to invest enough time with the person who is discouraged to be able to understand exactly what they are going through. Only then can you offer sincere hope with a genuine word of encouragement.

HELPER, COMFORTER, ENERGIZER

As a high-energy girl, I love the Greek word *parakletos*. It is a noun (related to *parakaleó*) which means "helper, comforter, energizer."

You are not meant to do life all alone. There are times when you will need a helper, a comforter, and definitely an energizer to help light a fire under you and rebuild your confidence when you are feeling discouraged. I enjoy getting to be that energizer for people, but I know there are times when I need it from others as well.

God desires for you to be that helper, comforter, and energizer for others when they need you, coming alongside of them with strength and encouragement.

Write about a time when you were a helper, comforter, or energizer for someone who needed encouragement:

In this world filled with despair and disappointments, we can all benefit from words of encouragement. God will always give you plenty of opportunities to be an encourager to others. All you have to do is be aware when you are connecting with people whether it is with the checker at the grocery store, your bank teller, your co-workers, or those with whom God has given you to build a deep relationship. When He provides those opportunities, take advantage of them and be sure you don't pass them up!

GOD'S PROVISION FOR ENCOURAGEMENT

Perhaps you have no one in your life who will come beside you to give you strength and encouragement when you need it most. God knows this and because He loves you deeply, He has provided for you in advance by giving you the Holy Spirit who will always be with you.

Jesus told His disciples that the Holy Spirit would be the Parakletos who would take His place after He ascended into heaven.

"If you love me, obey me; and I will ask the Father and he will give you another Comforter, and he will never leave you."

John 14:15-16 TLB

God has also gifted you with His Word, the Bible, to encourage you and give you hope. If you simply take the time to read it, you will receive a powerful boost for your spirit!

For everything that was written in the past was written to teach us, so that through the endurance taught in the Scriptures and the encouragement they provide we might have hope.

Romans 15:4

In what way has God encouraged you lately while reading His Word?

BE AN ENCOURAGER

An effective encourager is someone who has optimism, enthusiasm about life, and can relate to others in a positive way. They also radiate a quiet self-confidence, enabling them to be able to focus on others rather than demanding constant attention to fulfill their own emotional needs.

Whenever two people connect with each other, they will part either more encouraged or more discouraged. You have a choice with the kind of impact you will have on everyone you meet.

When God gives you a word to speak to someone who needs encouragement, be sure to listen to Him and share what He has given you to say. Be gracious with your words and don't hold back!

The gift of encouragement has been given to every one of us because it is God's desire for us to encourage others. But how often do we actually use that gift to build others up?

There are several ways we can easily encourage others…

SMILE

Sometimes, all it takes is a simple smile. A smile communicates affection, openness, and acceptance toward other people. It doesn't matter where you are in the world or what language you speak. A kind smile will always be understood.

When you smile, your body releases three hormones that make you feel good which include dopamine, endorphins, and serotonin. Likewise, when a person genuinely smiles at you, there is a feel-good boost to your spirit as well.

I have a dear friend who is so full of joy and smiles all the time. When I am around her, I can't help but smile more because her smile is so contagious! I love spending time with her because I feel so uplifted inside just from being around her. A smile is a great form of encouragement.

SEND AN EMAIL OR TEXT

Let someone know you are praying for them with an email or text which only takes a few minutes of your time. When you tell a person they are on your heart and that you have been prompted to pray for them, that is such a huge encouragement. The Holy Spirit is working on their behalf!

MAIL A CARD

Send a handwritten card in the mail with words of encouragement. I love receiving cards that warm my heart and lift my spirit. It is a rare practice in today's world of fast technology to send a card by snail mail, but what joy it brings to the heart to receive one! I have kept several encouraging letters, notes, and cards over the years because they meant so much to me to receive them.

A few years ago, I decided to practice being an encourager by sending out a handwritten card to a different person every week, all year long, with words that built them up in whatever way they needed it at that time in their life. Not surprisingly, God brought more than one person each week to my mind who needed encouragement.

It was such a blessing for me because it provided a huge boost to my spirit knowing I could play a part, whether big or small, in encouraging someone.

MEET IN PERSON

I find when I meet with someone in person, perhaps over a cup of coffee, I am able to spend more time being engaged in conversation and listening. That is when I can offer life-giving words to encourage because I have a deeper understanding of what is really going on in their life. And I am often encouraged by their words as well. God desires for us to spend quality time with each other for that very reason – to be able to encourage one another!

And let us not neglect our meeting together, as some people do, but encourage one another, especially now that the day of his return is drawing near.

Hebrews 10:25 NLT

A DIFFERENT KIND OF ENCOURAGEMENT

Parakaleó can also be a time of instructing, teaching, and even admonishing. Perhaps the person you are encouraging has journeyed off the path that they should be on to keep their relationship strong with the Lord.

You have the opportunity to say, with love, grace, and wisdom, what this person needs to hear – to encourage them to take action so they can get back on track with God. This is best done when you have face-to-face time with them…another reason to make time for that cup of coffee with the person in your life needing encouragement.

Have you ever experienced giving or receiving this kind of parakaleó encouragement? _____ In what way?

How did your friend react when you gave it?

How did you feel after receiving it?

The Apostle Paul set a great example for us by encouraging believers, telling them what they need to hear so they would change their behavior to live as God wanted them to live.

In this verse, parakaleó is translated as "beg:"

Therefore I, a prisoner for serving the Lord, beg you to lead a life worthy of your calling, for you have been called by God.

Ephesians 4:1 NLT

You may never know the impact you have on the life of someone you've encouraged, but God knows and will reward you in eternity for being a faithful encourager to others.

Discouragement is burdensome and can make the difficulties we go through in life feel incredibly overwhelming. Encouragement gives us the hope we need to get through those inevitable tough times. When we are energized for Christ, we can be an effective encourager, providing sweetness to the souls of those He has intended for us to meet on our journey in life.

And we can be confident in the promise that no matter what we go through, we have the greatest Encourager of all who will always be right by our side.

THE GIFT OF GRACE FOR A RADIANT LIFE

Because of the gift of God's grace in our lives and the encouragement of the Holy Spirit, we are able to season others with grace and encouragement as the salt of the earth through our words and actions for a radiant life.

Dear Heavenly Father,

Thank You for the gift of grace in my life. Please transform my heart to be more like You, eager to season others with grace as the salt of the earth. Please give me an attitude of humility, thankfulness, and forgiveness.

I pray that the words I speak would build others up and encourage them. Help me to find creative ways to effectively encourage those You have placed in my life. Thank You for providing the Holy Spirit to walk beside me as my loving and faithful Encourager, Helper, and Comforter.

In Jesus' name,

Amen

TAKE ACTION

Find a way to show grace to someone this week by putting their interests before your own, speaking kind words even when they seem undeserved, expressing thankfulness, giving a word of encouragement, being present for someone who is hurting, or forgiving a person who has wronged you. Then, take some time to journal your experience and how it helped you grow spiritually.

JOURNAL

LESSON FOUR

APRIL'S BIRTHSTONE: DIAMOND
The Gift of Clarity

LESSON FOUR
April's Birthstone: Diamond - The Gift of Clarity

KEY VERSE FOR A RADIANT LIFE

When Jesus spoke again to the people, he said, "I am the light of the world. Whoever follows me will never walk in darkness, but will have the light of life."

John 8:12

KINGDOM-FOCUSED CLARITY

People have been attracted to sparkle for hundreds of years. During the Georgian era, a period in British history from 1714 to 1830 during which the first four British monarchs of the House of Hanover reigned, a type of jewelry called "paste" became all the rage.

Paste is a type of glass which emulates precious stones. Hand-cut glass was placed on a metallic foil base, giving the effect similar to the glitter of diamonds. The foils were sometimes hand-tinted to imitate the color of other precious gemstones.

Paste had a pliable consistency, so craftsmen were able to use their creativity to make quite elaborate pieces with it. As the demand increased, glassmakers aspired to match the beautiful luster of diamonds.

A jeweler from Strasbourg named Georg Friedrich Strass was employed in Paris in 1724 and became famous for his version of paste jewelry. He substituted the foil with a metallic powder coating. It gave a mirror-like effect, reflecting back through the crystal which sparkled like a diamond when it came in contact with the light. He was so highly admired that he was appointed "Jeweler to the King." To this day, many refer to fine quality antique paste jewelry as "strass."

With each stone made by hand, the cost for paste jewelry remained high due to such slow production. Rhinestones soon replaced paste as a much more affordable alternative.

THE SPARKLE OF RHINESTONES

The name "rhinestone" came from the sparkling quartz pebbles that had been found on the banks of the Rhine River. Interestingly, this river forms the border of France and Germany where Strasbourg, Strass's hometown, is located.

These pebbles had a high lead content which gave them a brilliance well beyond the average quartz stone. Eventually, the river banks became depleted of them which inspired jewelers to create an imitation of this stone.

In 1895, a man named Daniel Swarovski had invented a new mechanized stone cutter to replace the time-consuming, hand-cut paste. It was now possible to produce large quantities of these faceted and polished glass gems with speed. He was intent on making them accessible to the greatest number of people with the vision of creating "a diamond for everyone." By the 1920s, Swarovski crystal jewelry was in demand around the world.

The desire for sparkle continued to pick up momentum. During the 1940s and '50s, vintage costume jewelry was made using these dazzling, high quality, crystal glass rhinestones.

Sparkling, colorless rhinestones are as close as one can get to resembling April's traditional birthstone, diamond, without the incredibly high price tag.

This is an example of a brilliant, colorless rhinestone vintage piece in my collection from the 1950s era:

APRIL'S BIRTHSTONE

Diamond, a chain of carbon atoms that have crystallized, is the hardest, naturally occurring mineral. It is found in igneous rock called kimberlite, a volcanic rock that is formed deep in the earth's crust as diamond can only be formed at high pressures.

 Diamond is found in approximately 35 countries including South Africa, Russia, and Botswana, the main producers of gem-quality diamond. They are also found in three states in the U.S…Arkansas, Colorado, and Wyoming.

If you ever want to mine for your own diamond, you can visit Crater of Diamonds State Park in Murfreesboro, Arkansas. It is the only publicly-owned mine. Since 1972, visitors have found over 33,000 diamonds including the largest diamond ever unearthed in the U.S. weighing 40.23 carats!

CUT AND CLARITY

The way a diamond is cut has the greatest influence on how much it will sparkle. This affects the quality. If the diamond has a poor cut, it may actually appear dull.

When a diamond is cut with proper proportions, light is returned out of the top of the diamond, also known as the table. If it is cut too shallow, light escapes out of the bottom. And when it is cut too deep, the light will seep out of the sides.

The cut of the diamond has three primary effects on its appearance. The first is *brilliance* which is the brightness created by the combination of the white light reflecting from the surface and from inside of the diamond. The second is *fire*, the dispersion of light into the colors of the visible spectrum which is seen as flashes of color. And the third is *scintillation*, the flashes of light and dark also known as sparkle when a diamond or the source of light hitting the diamond is moved.

Clarity, the visual appearance, is another universal method for assessing the quality of a diamond. Imperfections inside of the diamond are known as inclusions and those on the surface are called blemishes. The fewer imperfections there are the better the clarity, allowing the diamond to sparkle even more through the way it is cut.

CLARITY OF THE MIND

If you are a follower of Christ, clarity of the mind is vital for you to be able to truly sparkle as a reflection of Him. For true clarity, you must be kingdom-focused which gives you an eternal perspective on life, not temporal as this world was never meant to be our forever home. God has created an incredible place for us to live for all eternity if we accept Jesus as our Savior.

Set your minds on things that are above, not on things that are on earth.

Colossians 3:2 ESV

Just as the cut of the diamond has three significant effects on its appearance, there are three factors that affect keeping sparkling clarity for a kingdom focus…

CLARITY FACTOR #1

What do you allow to INFLUENCE your mind?

The Apostle Paul, in his letter to the Christians at Philippi, wrote:

Finally, brothers and sisters, whatever is true, whatever is noble, whatever is right, whatever is pure, whatever is lovely, whatever is admirable—if anything is excellent or praiseworthy—think about such things.

Philippians 4:8

The next time you sit down to watch television, try measuring what you are viewing against the standard of this Scripture. You will probably find it nearly impossible to find anything wholesome! I have noticed on most shows that are now being aired, God's name is continuously used in vain with complete disrespect and disregard for his holiness, and the morals portrayed are horribly corrupt.

The mind is a complex system that works much better the more you use it. Just as exercise for the body makes your muscles stronger, mental exercise makes the mind stronger. If you regularly watch hours of television or movies, your mind becomes stagnant, greatly diminishing your ability for creativity and imagination. Not only is it a waste of the limited time God gave you here on this earth to use for His glory, but it is also a waste of the mind.

What do you find is your biggest time-waster for your mind?

Instead of turning on the television, watching a movie, or scrolling through social media for more mind-numbing entertainment, use that time to open your Bible to fill your mind with all that is pure and praiseworthy so you will know how to live a life pleasing to God.

Give careful thought to the paths for your feet and be steadfast in all your ways.

Proverbs 4:26

Do not allow all the many influences of the world battling for your time to pull you off of the path God has planned for you. Rather, be guided by the One who wants the very best for you so you can experience, to the fullest, all of His incredible purposes for your life.

CLARITY FACTOR #2

What do you allow to CONTROL your mind?

The world offers an abundance of attractive, mind-controlling substances, many of which can become very addictive over time. Alcohol is one of the most acceptable of these substances in our society. However, drinking too much of it will affect your mind and your actions, taking complete control of you.

Don't drink too much wine, for many evils lie along that path; be filled instead with the Holy Spirit and controlled by him.

Ephesians 5:18 TLB

When you ask Jesus Christ to come into your life, you are given the wonderful and gracious gift of the Holy Spirit to help empower and guide you, leading you in the way you should go to be able to reflect Christ.

If alcohol is taking the place of the Holy Spirit when you drink more than you should, your decisions become controlled by alcohol, not by your Helper, the Holy Spirit. Clarity of thought becomes long gone as well as your focus on all that has eternal, kingdom value.

You have the choice of whether or not to accept guidance from the Holy Spirit. When you resist what He wants for you and give in to your desires to go your own way, it deeply grieves Him. Reading God's Word will help you recognize how the Holy Spirit is leading you.

He will never lead you to do anything contrary to God's Word. The same cannot be said of alcohol which will most likely lead you down a path of decision-making that continually opposes God's Word. If alcohol is a weakness for you, know that you do not have to struggle with it alone. The Holy Spirit promises to help you in your weakness. And God will give you the strength you need to live with complete clarity for a kingdom focus.

Likewise the Spirit helps us in our weakness. For we do not know what to pray for as we ought, but the Spirit himself intercedes for us with groanings too deep for words. And he who searches hearts knows what is the mind of the Spirit, because the Spirit intercedes for the saints according to the will of God.

Romans 8:26-27 ESV

What is a weakness hindering you from reflecting Christ that you need God's strength and power to overcome?

Isaiah describes God's incredible strength and power available to you:

"To whom will you compare me? Or who is my equal?" says the Holy One. Lift up your eyes and look to the heavens: Who created all these? He who brings out the starry host one by one and calls forth each of them by name. Because of his great power and mighty strength, not one of them is missing.

Isaiah 40:25-26

Do you not know? Have you not heard? The LORD is the everlasting God, the Creator of the ends of the earth. He will not grow tired or weary, and his understanding no one can fathom. He gives strength to the weary and increases the power of the weak.

Isaiah 40:28-29

Your powerful Creator who has named each star in the sky loves you and cares about you personally. He deeply desires to give you the strength and power you need to overcome anything controlling you that reduces your clarity of the mind and kingdom focus.

CLARITY FACTOR #3

What do you allow to DISTRACT your mind?

Natural diamonds originate as a result of carbon exposed to intense heat and pressure deep in the earth. This process can cause irregular crystals, otherwise known as inclusions, to become trapped inside of the diamond while it is forming. These can greatly reduce the clarity of the diamond.

The more time you spend thinking about God and what He values, the more it becomes a natural state of mind, increasing your clarity. However, your focus will become blurred when you keep your mind set on things that only have earthly value – the temporary, distracting things of this life that will one day all be destroyed. You will then bring on more worry and anxiety, creating inclusions that lower your clarity and reflect less of Christ's light in you.

What gives you worry and anxiety in your life?

The answer to staying kingdom-focused is spending more time with God in His presence which you are designed to do. He desires closeness with you! This will help reduce those inclusions (worry and anxiety) that are clouding your clarity, replacing them with His perfect peace.

Don't worry about anything; instead, pray about everything. Tell God what you need, and thank him for all he has done. Then you will experience God's peace, which exceeds anything we can understand. His peace will guard your hearts and minds as you live in Christ Jesus.

Philippians 4:6-7 NLT

What does God promise to give you in exchange for your worry?

If your clarity has become blurred over time from all that you have allowed to influence, control, and distract your mind, know that there is hope. God is the Master of transformation. He can bring perfect clarity to a mind that has completely lost its brightness.

PERFECT VISION THROUGH THE LIGHT OF THE WORLD

It was an East Dallas home tour weekend with several charming mid-century moderns on the list. Michael and I registered early and cleared our schedules to be able to go. Since we had recently bought an updated home built in 1950, we both enjoyed seeing the way others remodeled and decorated their mid-century homes using inspiring creativity.

There was one particular home on this tour that I will never forget…

As we entered one of the bedrooms, I noticed a large walk-in closet with a wide-open door. It felt like an invitation, so I curiously poked my head inside. I was astonished to see that every piece of clothing hanging up was black!

At first, I thought they must all be uniforms. But when I took a closer look, the tops and bottoms were very different – not uniforms at all. I thought to myself, *Who would ever want to wear only the color black? How depressing!*

Now, this is coming from someone whose closet is packed with color – and lots of it. I just didn't get it. Until I spoke with a friend who used to wear black. And only black.

COLOR PSYCHOLOGY

Every color of the spectrum has a bit of psychology tied to it. We are drawn to specific colors for a reason. Each color has an association with a reaction in our brain when we internalize it.

My favorite color, for example, is orange. It represents enthusiasm, creativity, and determination, all a huge part of my personality. I see orange and I am completely magnetized toward it.

The color black is the absorption of all color and the absence of light. Black is a color that hides. It can be used to hide things such as emotions, insecurities, or even as a slimming color to hide weight. My friend's reason for wearing it, she told me, was to try to hide the pain of her past and her overwhelming sadness that she experienced throughout much of her life.

MOURNING IN BLACK

Black also expresses grief. We often select this somber color to wear when attending a funeral. Back in the Victorian era, women actually did not have a choice to wear any color *but* black for a minimum of two years after their husband passed.

The Victorian era started in 1837 when Victoria became the Queen of England at the age of 18. She was young, pretty, and quite admired throughout the land. Whatever she wore became the latest fashion trend.

In 1840, she married her first cousin Prince Albert. After 21 years of marriage and nine children, her beloved Prince Albert died at age 42 of typhoid fever. The Queen then went into a deep depression and mourning, dressing only in the color black for the remainder of her life.

When a widow of Victorian society was in deep mourning, she was expected to wear clothing made entirely of black crepe, a dull fabric that had no sheen so as not to reflect any light.

After one year of deep mourning, a widow would go into half-mourning and could wear black silk. After two years of mourning were over, widows could freely wear any color. However, many imitated Queen Victoria and wore black for the rest of their lives.

It is your choice whether or not you want to wear light or dark clothing. But did you know it is also your choice to invite the light into your heart, mind, and spirit that God offers to guide you out of your darkness? We all start out in darkness with a sin nature, but if you decide to stay there you will become spiritually blind.

Spiritual blindness is the inability to see God because of a lack of belief in Him and in His Word. To remain in your blindness is insisting that you can see perfectly fine on your own with no need for a Savior. That is called pride. He will leave you in your blindness because you are rejecting His grace to give you the eyes to see and the mind to understand His truth.

Pride hinders your spiritual sight because you put your faith in your own ability to do things that are beyond your strength. It comes from having too high of an opinion of yourself. You need God's help. The moment you humble yourself and ask Him to help you see, He gives you His light and you no longer have to walk in darkness.

When Jesus spoke again to the people, he said, "I am the light of the world. Whoever follows me will never walk in darkness, but will have the light of life."

John 8:12

Often times, if a person's life is consumed with their sin, they will not go anywhere near the light because their sin will be exposed. Rejecting the light that God offers to lead you out of your blindness results in a further hardening of your heart in unbelief. It slowly becomes more and more difficult to see, hear, and comprehend the truth.

Have you ever found yourself in a place where you were spiritually blind, unwilling to see the truth about the sin in your life?

The Apostle Paul found this to be true when he spoke to some of the Jewish leaders…

And after they had argued back and forth among themselves, they left with this final word from Paul: "The Holy Spirit was right when he said to your ancestors through Isaiah the prophet, 'Go and say to this people: When you hear what I say, you will not understand. When you see what I do, you will not comprehend. For the hearts of these people are hardened, and their ears cannot hear, and they have closed their eyes—so their eyes cannot see, and their ears cannot hear, and their hearts cannot understand, and they cannot turn to me and let me heal them.'

Acts 28:25-27 NLT

DELIVERED FROM DARKNESS

Why are there so many spiritually blind people all around us?

Satan, the god of this world, is desperately fighting to keep anyone he can from being able to understand God's truth, see His light, and experience His grace. He wants to keep people from hearing the Good News…the news that they can be completely forgiven of all their sins and live in freedom. If he can do that, he knows they will stay in bondage to their sin.

Satan is the ruler of darkness and would love nothing more than to rule over as many people as possible, holding them captive in total darkness with him. And he has been successful with quite a large number of them.

Satan, who is the god of this world, has blinded the minds of those who don't believe. They are unable to see the glorious light of the Good News. They don't understand this message about the glory of Christ, who is the exact likeness of God.

2 Corinthians 4:4 NLT

It is only by the power of God and His grace that you can be delivered from this darkness. When you make God the Ruler of your life, He protects you from the god of this world, keeping you in the light and taking away the veil, your spiritual blindness, so you can understand His liberating truths.

But whenever someone turns to the Lord, the veil is taken away.

2 Corinthians 3:16 NLT

If you want strong, spiritual vision you must take action. Spending time regularly talking to God and taking time to listen to Him by reading what He has to say to you through His Word will deepen your relationship. It is a relationship that begins here on earth and will continue into eternity.

You will slowly begin to see your blindness fade away. And it will be replaced with razor-sharp, unobstructed spiritual vision - something we all greatly need if we are to stay out of the darkness and live a life of freedom offered to us by our gracious Savior, the Light of the world.

THE GIFT OF CLARITY FOR A RADIANT LIFE

The gift of clarity provides perfect vision to help you focus on that which has eternal value so you can live a radiant life that will sparkle brightly for Christ.

Dear Heavenly Father,

Thank You for the gift of clarity and the ability to have perfect spiritual vision so I can stay out of the darkness and live in Your light. Please help me to keep an eternal perspective on life so I will remain kingdom-focused.

I pray that I will make good decisions that please You with everything I allow to influence, control, and distract my mind. Please keep me from being spiritually blind and my heart humble so I can be aware of the sin in my life and live in Your freedom. Thank You for Your promise that if I follow You, I will have the light of life.

In Jesus' name,

Amen

TAKE ACTION

Think about the choices you make with all that you allow to influence, control, and distract your mind. What changes need to be made to increase the clarity of your mind?

For incredible sparkle that reflects the light of Christ, set a new standard to allow into your mind only that which is true, noble, right, pure, lovely, admirable, excellent, or praiseworthy. Journal the way the changes you make affect the clarity of your mind.

LESSON FIVE

MAY'S BIRTHSTONE: EMERALD
The Gift of Rest

LESSON FIVE

May's Birthstone: Emerald - The Gift of Rest

KEY VERSE FOR A RADIANT LIFE

The LORD is my shepherd; I shall not want. He makes me lie down in green pastures. He leads me beside still waters. He restores my soul.

Psalm 23:1-2 ESV

GREEN: GOD'S COLOR FOR REST AND RENEWAL

Imagine living in a world without color. How incredibly dull and dreary that would be! Thankfully, we have a Creator with an amazing imagination who gave us color everywhere we look.

Research has shown that color can affect the mind, body, and spirit. For example, red stimulates the mind, quickly grabbing our attention such as when we see a red traffic light. This creates a reaction by the body to step on the brake.

Blue has a calming effect. If you lie on your back and spend some time staring up at a clear, blue sky, you will most likely begin to feel a sense of peace come over you and your body will relax.

Green is a soothing and healing color. Grass green is considered the most restful color for the human eye. Being in the center of the color spectrum, no adjustment is required by the eyes when seeing green and is therefore considered restful. Perhaps that is why May's traditional green birthstone, the emerald, has been one of the most desirable and valuable colored gemstones for over 5,000 years!

MAY'S BIRTHSTONE

Emerald is a treasured, green stone and one of the four precious gemstones which also include diamond, ruby, and sapphire. It is a variety of the mineral beryl with its green color coming from trace amounts of chromium or vanadium. To be classified as a "fine emerald," the hue must be saturated with a vivid, verdant green and it must also be highly transparent.

Emerald is a weaker stone because of its many inclusions (imperfections). This creates a challenge when cutting the stone for making jewelry. Emeralds without inclusions are rare and much more difficult to find, making their worth much higher than diamonds. An emerald's value is also determined by carat weight, color, cut, and clarity.

Between 50 and 90% of the world's emeralds come out of Columbia. Emeralds are found all over the world in many other countries such as Austria, Ethiopia, Madagascar, and Zambia. They have also been mined in the U.S. in Connecticut, Montana, Nevada, and the Carolinas.

I have been able to find that rich, emerald green color in the rhinestones of several pieces of vintage costume jewelry I've collected from the Golden Era of the 1940s and '50s.

This is one of my favorites, surrounded by colorless rhinestones so sparkly it appears as if it was never worn:

GREEN IS ALL AROUND US

The next time you step outside, stop and take a look around. You will notice that the color green appears in nature more than any other color. Plants of all kinds are clothed in various shades of green because of a pigment in their cells called chlorophyll. I do not think it was a coincidence that God provided so much green around us outdoors.

Green is known to renew and restore depleted energy as a restful sanctuary, away from all of the stress we encounter in our busy lives. Relaxing in a green environment restores us back to a sense of well-being. God knew how much we would need that in the 21st century!

The 24 hours we are given each day never seem to be enough to accomplish everything we want or need to do. We just rapidly keep moving from one task to the next, creating this feeling of being overworked and severely stressed.

The Psalmist David was in need of de-stressing as well and wrote a beautiful Psalm about how God renews and restores us in nature.

These are the first few lines of it:

The LORD is my shepherd; I shall not want. He makes me lie down in green pastures. He leads me beside still waters. He restores my soul.

Psalm 23:1-2 ESV

Another way of saying it is like this:

Because the Lord is my Shepherd, I have everything I need. He lets me rest in the healing nature He created for me which gives me renewed strength. He helps me live a life that brings Him honor and glorifies His name.

What a wonderful gift from our Creator who knows exactly what we need!

MENTAL BENEFITS OF REST

Americans spend approximately 50% of their waking hours devoted to work. And when we are not working, our brains are totally preoccupied with it. Our mental resources are continuously being depleted throughout the day.

But there is good news! Many studies have shown that rest and downtime can replenish those reserves while restoring our attention and motivation. Downtime also encourages productivity and creativity. When the brain is not learning something new, it can secure data recently learned and etch new skills into the brain. So many good reasons to take the time to rest!

Do you give yourself enough rest and downtime? _____

As much as it is God's desire for us to work using our unique skills with which He blessed us, it is also His desire for us to have regular rest for our mind, body, and spirit away from our work.

He set the standard for rest after he created the world in six days and then rested on the seventh day:

By the seventh day God had finished the work he had been doing; so on the seventh day he rested from all his work. Then God blessed the seventh day and made it holy, because on it he rested from all the work of creating that he had done.

Genesis 2:2-3

PHYSICAL BENEFITS OF REST

According to the Environmental Protection Agency (EPA), the average American spends 93% of their life indoors. One of the best ways to recharge is to go to a place where you are outdoors, surrounded by nature with lots of green which has a restorative, healing effect.

It allows your brain to wander, rest, and recover from the wired world of digital communication and the frenzied pace and noise around you. There is a sense of peace you feel when you are in nature and far away from a stressful environment.

A study from 2012, published in the journal *Landscape and Urban Planning*, discovered that adults who lived in places with the most amount of green space felt less stress and experienced lower levels of cortisol, the stress hormone that plays a role in our fight or flight response.

When cortisol is too high for too long, it can increase the amount of fat you hold in your abdomen (visceral fat) which increases your risk for heart disease. That seems to be a good enough reason right there to motivate all of us to take time each day to be in nature!

How often do you take time to be outdoors?

_____ often

_____ sometimes

_____ rarely

If you find yourself exhausted from overworking, be sure to make necessary changes in your life before you are forced to rest due to serious health consequences. Consider taking an extended period of rest, otherwise known as a vacation!

Where do you like to get away for a vacation and why?

Make it a priority to have an escape from your regular routine of responsibilities at least once a year. With a rested and refreshed mind and body, you will be more open to all the new ways God wants to use your gifts for His glory.

SPIRITUAL BENEFITS OF REST

Why does God value rest for His children so much? One reason is that He wants us to reflect Him by shining with His light so that others will be drawn to Him. When we share His love and goodness with others through our actions, He is glorified.

If you are always exhausted from constant work and busyness, how are you going to be able to shine brightly for Him? In the same way that it takes energy to power a light bulb, it also takes energy to shine for Christ. Rest will renew your energy needed to be able to do that.

In the same way, let your light shine before others, that they may see your good deeds and glorify your Father in heaven.

Matthew 5:16

Another reason God desires for us to have proper rest is that when we are too busy and distracted without any downtime, we can end up tuning God out of our lives whether we realize it or not. We blindly walk in one direction or another, not having any idea about the path we are to be on to experience His very best for us.

All of your time and energy can end up being focused on things that do not have any eternal, kingdom value, causing you to miss out on some of the most amazing blessings God has had planned for you. Be sure to make time for God, away from the busyness of your life to hear His voice.

God speaks most clearly to us through His Word, so make it a priority to read His words of guidance in the Bible daily, asking Him to direct every step you take on your journey in life. He delights in being involved, even in the smallest details!

The LORD directs the steps of the godly. He delights in every detail of their lives.

Psalm 37:23 NLT

How often do you share the details of what is going on in your life with God?

_____ often

_____ sometimes

_____ rarely

I love spending time with God on my walks outside, surrounded by nature. I find that is a perfect way for me to share, reflect, and listen to what God might be trying to tell me.

When you are in need of refreshment for your mind, body, and spirit, find an area to walk where you are surrounded by the restful, green beauty that God has lovingly created for you and relax in the truth of Jesus' healing words:

"Come to me, all of you who are weary and carry heavy burdens, and I will give you rest. Take my yoke upon you. Let me teach you, because I am humble and gentle at heart, and you will find rest for your souls. For my yoke is easy to bear, and the burden I give you is light."

Matthew 11:28-30 NLT

What are some of your heavy burdens that you need to give to God?

RESTED, REFRESHED, AND READY TO SERVE

Running through the sprinklers, swimming with friends at the community pool, church camp, Mom's homemade popsicles, shucking corn and snapping beans from the garden with Dad, juicy watermelon, slip and slides, and at least one good, long road trip.

Ahhh…the sweet memories of childhood summers!

When I was a kid, I lived for summer. With no homework to be done and not a single care in the world, it was VACATION from the moment the last school bell rang until starting back up again in September.

For kids, summer is a season filled with hours and hours of freedom to play hard and just relax. They do not weigh the pros and cons of how they are spending their time or think about whether or not they should be more productive. They just enjoy life!

Something shifts, though, when we reach adulthood. For many of us, it feels foolish to "waste" time by goofing off or relaxing too much. As adults, we have created a frantic lifestyle where every minute counts. We are impatient if we have to wait for anything. Time is money.

In our efforts to accumulate bigger, better, and nicer things, we spend all of our time working away at our job six, and sometimes even seven, days a week. There is very little rest for our minds and bodies as we push ourselves to work harder and harder. We strive to be continuously productive, making good use of every moment. Paid time off goes unused and vacations become few and far between.

When vacations are taken, many of us would never dream of leaving home without our laptops, cell phones, and other technical gadgets that keep us "plugged in" to work, social media, the news, and other things that cause us a lot of stress. Sadly, summer is just another season.

SERVE GOD BY SERVING OTHERS

Without a proper balance between work and rest, there are serious consequences. Decades of research supporting the 40-hour work week show that working longer can increase your risk of chronic stress, major depression, and heart disease. You become more prone to skipping your workouts, eating foods that are not as healthy for you, skimping on sleep, and spending less time with the people who matter most to you.

What unhealthy habits do you tend to pick up when you work too much?

When you have a good balance of work and rest, you are better able to do what you were ultimately designed to do…to serve God by serving others. It takes energy to serve, so it is essential to set aside one day each week to rest your mind and body from working. Think of it as pausing your shallow work one day a week for God's deep work.

God has gifted you with unique talents and special skills. Rather than working every waking moment to accumulate more and more for yourself, God wants you to take time to rest and be refreshed so you can use your gifts energetically to show His love and grace to others through serving. It is a way of expressing gratitude for all He has done for you.

Each of you should use whatever gift you have received to serve others, as faithful stewards of God's grace in its various forms.

1 Peter 4:10

In what ways do you serve others as a faithful steward of God's grace?

When you have a relationship with God, you will want to serve Him as a natural, love-filled response. The more you know Him by spending time with Him in His Word and realize how much He loves you, the more you will want to please Him.

As followers of Christ, we are to strive to be more like Him. Jesus was a true servant throughout His life on earth and even in His death for us.

"For even the Son of Man came not to be served but to serve others and to give his life as a ransom for many."

Matthew 20:28 NLT

SERVING BENEFITS THE MIND, BODY, AND SPIRIT

Studies have shown that volunteering helps people who give of their time to feel more socially connected which lowers the risk of loneliness and depression.

A person's physical health may also be rewarded by serving others. A four-year study between 2006 and 2010 was published in *Psychology and Aging* and found that adults 50+ who volunteered on a regular basis were less likely to develop high blood pressure than non-volunteers. Blood pressure is a very important indicator of health because when it is elevated, it increases your risk of heart disease, stroke, and premature death.

Do you currently volunteer your time? _____ If so, what do you do?

Another benefit of serving is that God increases our faith by showing us our potential. Seeing what God can do when His power is at work within us gives us the confidence to do even more for Him and to look for new doors He is opening for us to serve others with our gifts.

A few years ago, I was asked to teach a Bible study with a group of women at Exodus, a ministry that "empowers formerly incarcerated mothers and their children to achieve a productive and fulfilling life through Jesus Christ."

They fulfill this mission statement of theirs by giving the women a place to live with their children for one full year, teaching them vital parenting, employment, and relationship skills as well as money management and biblical principles.

The Bible study I was asked to teach was *Beauty in a Life Repurposed* which they learned I had recently written and published.

It was an open door for me to use my gifts of writing and teaching to serve. I was so blessed through my experience with these women and it gave me the confidence I needed to teach my Bible study to many other groups of women that followed as God continued to open other new doors.

Where has God opened the door for you to be able to use your gifts to serve?

SERVING IS AN INVESTMENT IN ETERNITY

When you take time to serve others, you may not see the results of your hard work right away, but you are planting seeds of generosity which will produce a generous harvest one day for eternity.

Remember this: Whoever sows sparingly will also reap sparingly, and whoever sows generously will also reap generously.

2 Corinthians 9:6

Know that you are making a difference by investing in people who may come to know Christ through you because of the love you have shown them by serving. In time, either here on earth or in eternity, your blessings will be overflowing.

THE GIFT OF REST FOR A RADIANT LIFE

Take time for the gift of rest so you can renew your energy to serve others, sharing God's love while shining brightly for Him. Give yourself downtime each day to spend with God so you can be refreshed to hear His voice as He directs you on your journey as a faithful steward of His grace for a radiant life.

Dear Heavenly Father,

Thank You for the gift of rest You offer for my mind, body, and spirit. Please help me to be more balanced between work and rest so I can have more energy to share Your love and goodness through serving others. I pray that I will be ready to walk through any new doors You open for me, using my gifts to bring You glory. Thank You for providing an environment of rest for my soul in the beauty of nature.

In Jesus' name,

Amen

TAKE ACTION

Look at the week ahead and schedule downtime each day to be in nature so your mind, body, and spirit have a chance to recharge. Take your Bible with you and spend some time in God's presence and in His Word. Journal all He is teaching you during your time with Him. Continue to schedule a break for refreshment each day to renew your energy.

LESSON SIX

JUNE'S BIRTHSTONE: PEARL
The Gift of Purity

LESSON SIX
June's Birthstone: Pearl - The Gift of Purity

KEY VERSE FOR A RADIANT LIFE

Blessed is the one whose transgressions are forgiven, whose sins are covered.

Psalm 32:1

MORE PRECIOUS THAN PEARLS

Jean de La Bruyère (1645 - 1696), a French philosopher and moralist, once said, "The rarest things in the world, next to a spirit of discernment, are diamonds and pearls."

When I first read this quote I understood the rarity of having a spirit of discernment, but I must admit I was a bit confused that this philosopher would describe pearls as being one of the "rarest things in the world."

How can that be? We see them displayed on jewelry counters throughout department stores sitting right out in the open for anyone to try on. Just about anywhere you go, women accessorize with pearls whether it is a wedding, funeral, bridal or baby shower, or simply dressing up for a day at the office. As Jackie Kennedy remarked about June's traditional birthstone, "Pearls are always appropriate."

JUNE'S BIRTHSTONE

After doing a bit of research on pearls, I found it is the natural pearls that grow on their own in the wild without the help of being farmed that are extremely rare. Only one in about 10,000 wild oysters will produce a pearl. Of those, only a very small number will have a desirable size, shape, and color for the jewelry industry.

The finest quality of natural pearls are highly valued as gemstones. Some natural pearls have been valued as high as $300,000 for a single pearl!

In December of 2015, an extraordinary strand of 45 white to light cream graduated natural pearls became available at an auction in Boston. The strand had come from the collection of a prominent British American family and had been purchased during the late 1800s. It ended up selling for the astonishing price of $2,211,000! These rare, natural pearls were definitely regarded as valuable.

Up until the beginning of the 20th century, the only way to harvest pearls was for divers to risk their lives by descending at depths of up to 100 feet to retrieve oysters. It was a dangerous job with very limited success as thousands of oysters would deliver only a mere three or four quality pearls.

Cultured or farmed pearls from pearl oysters are the majority of what is sold today and come from China.

THE FORMATION OF A PEARL

A pearl is formed when a microscopic intruder or parasite enters a mollusk with a hinged shell and settles between the shell and mantle, the protective layer that covers the mollusk's organs to keep it alive.

The mollusk becomes irritated by this potentially threatening intruder. As a defense mechanism, a fluid is secreted to coat the threatening irritant sealing off the irritation. This coating is called nacre, a crystalline substance known as mother of pearl that creates the iridescence seen in pearls.

Over time (between six months and four years), after several layers are deposited to produce a thick layer of nacre, a lustrous pearl is formed. The luster is the quantity and quality of light reflected from the pearl's surface. The higher the luster, the longer the durability and life of the pearl.

Ideally, the pearl will be perfectly round and smooth (most valuable) but the final outcome can have a variety of shapes.

I have found a few pearl beauties during my treasure hunts for vintage costume jewelry. This is a pretty floral design with pearls and gold in my collection from the 1960s era:

Natural pearls are rare but as Jean de La Bruyère expressed, a spirit of discernment is the rarest. Discernment is the ability to clearly comprehend and distinguish between that which is right or wrong, truth or error. It is the ability to see what is not evident to the average mind.

More than a thousand years earlier, King Solomon also knew how rare and valuable it was to have a spirit of discernment when he made his request to God:

"Now, LORD my God, you have made your servant king in place of my father David. But I am only a little child and do not know how to carry out my duties. Your servant is here among the people you have chosen, a great people, too numerous to count or number. So give your servant a discerning heart to govern your people and to distinguish between right and wrong. For who is able to govern this great people of yours?"

The LORD was pleased that Solomon had asked for this. So God said to him, "Since you have asked for this and not for long life or wealth for yourself, nor have asked for the death of your enemies but for discernment in administering justice, I will do what you have asked. I will give you a wise and discerning heart, so that there will never have been anyone like you, nor will there ever be.

Moreover, I will give you what you have not asked for—both wealth and honor—so that in your lifetime you will have no equal among kings. And if you walk in obedience to me and keep my decrees and commands as David your father did, I will give you a long life."

I Kings 3:7-14

King Solomon was humble and knew about his own deficiency in being able to discern right from wrong. He asked the Lord specifically for help in that area and God was pleased with his request, giving him exactly what he asked for and then so much more as an added blessing.

The Apostle Paul wrote about how it is the responsibility of every follower of Christ to be spiritually discerning so we can live a life of purity:

But examine everything carefully; hold fast to that which is good; abstain from every form of evil.

1 Thessalonians 5:21-22 NASB

Write about a time when God gave you spiritual discernment:

KNOW THE TRUTH IN A PERSONAL WAY

Spiritual discernment comes from knowing Jesus Christ in a real and personal way. Discernment is developed by becoming proficient in the Word of God by regularly studying Scripture. These are God's words written to us to teach us how to distinguish truth from error. The more we read it, the more we become acquainted with it, reinforcing the truth. And the more intimately we know Christ who is Truth, the easier it is to recognize when something is inaccurate or untrue.

This reminds me of some of the "signed" costume jewelry that I have seen for sale. There are numerous reproductions of vintage pieces of jewelry made by some of the most talented designers. They even include the stamped signature!

If you have not studied the designer and the way they skillfully made their jewelry, it can be difficult to discern between what is authentic and what is a fake. The more I study the designer and the materials they used for their jewelry, the easier it is for me to recognize the real deal.

When you desire to know the truth, you are desiring a life free from compromise that would pollute your character. You want to live a life of purity and integrity reflecting the real deal, Jesus Christ.

Another way spiritual discernment is developed is through the regular practice of identifying good from evil. We learn through experience what is pleasing to God, distinguishing His voice over the world's voice telling us what is right and wrong.

But solid food is for the mature, for those who have their powers of discernment trained by constant practice to distinguish good from evil.

Hebrews 5:14 ESV

Our senses become improved over time. What is good, true, and right tastes sweet to us and what is evil, false, and wrong has a very bitter taste. This protects us from the hurt and pain that comes from making decisions that do not glorify God and cause us to sin.

The closer our relationship to God, the more we will want to please Him by obeying Him and doing what is right. Our Creator deeply desires to have a close relationship with us and freely gives us a spirit of discernment anytime we ask. When we make decisions that honor Him, we end up prospering with abundant blessing!

Blessed is the one who does not walk in step with the wicked or stand in the way that sinners take or sit in the company of mockers, but whose delight is in the law of the Lord, and who meditates on his law day and night. That person is like a tree planted by streams of water, which yields its fruit in season and whose leaf does not wither— whatever they do prospers.

Psalm 1:1-3

Do you remember a time when you made a decision that honored God and were blessed because of it?

The next time you see someone wearing pearls, remember the way they are formed. Imagine yourself as a pearl sitting inside of a protective, hinged mollusk.

The numerous translucent layers of nacre that make up the pearl as it is being formed are like the layers of discernment you receive as you become closer in your relationship with Christ. Over time, these layers create a beautiful, iridescent luster. The more layers, the finer the luster allowing for a greater reflection of light in the pearl.

When you have a spirit of discernment, you brilliantly reflect Christ in your life as you make decisions that please and honor Him. And that is, by far, more precious than the rarest of natural pearls.

AN UNBLEMISHED ENTRANCE INTO ETERNITY

The pearl has a long and fascinating history. It is the oldest known gem and was considered the most valuable for centuries. It is also a symbol of unblemished perfection. The meaning of the Latin word for pearl is "unique" as no two pearls are ever exactly alike.

All over the world, pearls have been esteemed as precious and valuable. As early as 2300 BC, pearls were presented as gifts to Chinese royalty. In ancient Rome, which began in 753 BC, pearl jewelry was considered the ultimate status symbol. Pearls were considered so precious that Julius Caesar passed a law in the first century BC limiting the wearing of pearls to only the ruling classes.

Long before the discovery of oil, the Persian Gulf was at the center of the pearl trade which created a great source of wealth in the region. In Western Europe, ladies of nobility and royalty wore very elaborate pearl jewelry which created an insatiable desire for pearls. By the 19th century, the demand for pearl jewelry became so high that oyster supplies began to diminish.

HEAVEN'S GATES

The Apostle John was given a vision of the new heaven and the new earth described for us by him in the Bible throughout the book of Revelation. After knowing what I now know about pearls, I must admit, the description of the gates is difficult for my human mind to fathom!

The twelve gates were twelve pearls, each gate made of a single pearl.

Revelation 21:21a

Can you imagine each gate made of just one single pearl? What an awesome sight that will be as we enter into our eternal Home!

These pearl gates will always be open because there is no night there. Normally, a city's gates are open during the day and closed at night to protect against enemy attack. But because there is no night and no enemy to fear, the gates will always be open.

On no day will its gates ever be shut, for there will be no night there.

Revelation 21:25

As a symbol of unblemished perfection, it is not surprising that the gates are made of pearls as nothing impure will ever be allowed to enter through them. Thankfully, God made a way for every one of us to enter even though we are sinners, far from unblemished!

Just like the nacre covers the irritant in the mollusk for protection, Jesus covers our sin with His shed blood, the highest price He could pay, so we can be pure and holy, protected to be able to enter through those perfect pearl gates into our eternal Home.

Blessed is the one whose transgression is forgiven, whose sin is covered.

Psalm 32:1

ENTERING THROUGH THE PEARL GATES

Although everyone is welcome to enter through these pearl gates, not everyone will. There is one simple requirement which is to accept Jesus' gracious, merciful, and loving invitation to be with Him for eternity by acknowledging He is your Savior – that He alone can save you.

"For God so loved the world, that he gave his only Son, that whoever believes in him should not perish but have eternal life."

John 3:16

If you have accepted His invitation, your sins are wiped away forever and your name is permanently written in the Lamb's book of life. As one who is unblemished and pure, you will be free to enter through those breathtaking pearl gates when you pass from this temporary life on earth into your eternal Home!

Have you acknowledged that Jesus Christ is your Savior? _____

Nothing impure will ever enter it, nor will anyone who does what is shameful or deceitful, but only those whose names are written in the Lamb's book of life.

Revelation 21:27

Yes, those natural pearls are extremely valuable. But you are far more valuable to God. You are His child, created to be completely unique and unlike anyone else in the whole world. He paid the highest price to be with you for eternity by giving His life, shedding His blood so all of your deepest, darkest sins could be completely covered with His radiant light and flawless purity. Like the beautiful, lustrous nacre of a precious pearl.

SECURE IN YOUR SELF-WORTH

One of the posts on social media that I've seen more frequently than others lately is the one that says, "You are enough." I even saw a sign, created to remind me I was *more* than enough.

Our self-worth has been tested on a daily basis. We are constantly made to feel like we could be doing better when compared to others or that we could have accomplished a whole lot more by now. The media is to blame as well, claiming we must have beauty, wealth, intelligence, and success to be somebody who really matters.

Every person on the planet needs to know that they matter. They need to feel valued and that they mean something to someone. To see the words "You are enough" or "You are more than enough" feels comforting.

But is it true? Are we really enough?

DEAD IN SINS, ALIVE IN CHRIST

We were made in the image of God as an expression of His glory, beautifully created by the Master Artist and knit together with so much love in our mother's womb. God had a wonderful plan mapped out for our lives before we took our first breath.

When we came into the world, we were meant to live in perfect harmony with God. But our sin caused us to become distorted versions of ourselves with limitations, flaws, and weaknesses.

The Bible tells us that before we surrender to Him, we are dead in our sins. Is there any worth in something that is dead? None at all.

Jesus took our sin upon Himself on the cross, not because we were worthy in any way but because there was no possible way we ourselves could become worthy or alive on our own. We are far from "enough."

But because of his great love for us, God, who is rich in mercy, made us alive with Christ even when we were dead in transgressions—it is by grace you have been saved.

Ephesians 2:4-5

When we give our lives to Jesus, His grace transforms us from lifeless to fully alive as a new creation in Christ who will live for eternity with Him!

Therefore, if anyone is in Christ, he is a new creation; the old has passed away, behold, the new has come.

2 Corinthians 5:17 NASB

As a new creation in Christ, what desires from your old sin nature seem to have passed away?

He made us righteous – completely pure and blameless in His sight, giving us immeasurable worth because of the price He paid through His sacrifice on the cross.

God made him who had no sin to be sin for us, so that in him we might become the righteousness of God.

2 Corinthians 5:21

When God instills His worth in us, it outweighs any sense of self-worth we could try to instill in ourselves no matter how successful, wealthy, beautiful, or intelligent we are. We will never be enough on our own. He is the reason for any and all of our self-worth. He is more than enough for us!

MODERN IDOLATRY

There is a serious danger we face when replacing a biblical view of our self-worth with a worldly view. For many of us, physical appearance becomes the focus. We're obsessed with looking younger and younger. Excessive time, money, and energy are spent on becoming more attractive in the world's eyes just so we can feel like we have self-worth.

According to a report from the retail analytics firm Edited, the beauty industry was valued at $532 billion last year (2019) and is on a rapid upward trajectory.

When there is something that is loved, desired, and enjoyed more than God, it becomes idolatry. Being satisfied by anything we treasure more than Him starts in the heart. These desires only get stronger the more we indulge in them.

The Apostle Paul warned the church at Corinth, a city that was full of idols, by saying:

Therefore, my dear friends, flee from idolatry.

1 Corinthians 10:14

You may think of idolatry as worship of a statue or image as practiced back in Bible times. Today, we have modern idolatry which looks a little different but is the same idea. Instead of bowing before a carved object, we look for other things to "worship" – to give all of our efforts and energy to boost our self-worth, taking the place of God in our lives.

Appearance is just one of many. Other examples of things we use to try to make us feel worthy are success, money, pleasure, beauty, luxury items, and relationships. When used for the purpose of feeling worthy, the one thing they all have in common is the building up of one's self. So the basis of modern idolatry is actually the worship of self.

What comes to mind that has or could easily become idolatry in your life?

SEEKING SELF-WORTH

Attempting to create our self-worth on our own is prideful. It is implying that we think we can do a better job than God or that what He has provided for our self-worth is not enough.

We will never find fulfillment seeking to build up our self-worth on our own. All of the meaningless things for which we strive and the world's admiration of them will be of no use to us after we die because these are all things that have no eternal value.

Jesus knew we would struggle with idolatry to fill a void and to try to make ourselves feel better inside, but He also knew these things would only lead to emptiness and self-worth that would never measure up to the world's standards no matter how hard we try.

Only God deserves our deepest affections and admiration. He alone gives us our true self-worth that completely satisfies. When you love God with all your heart, soul, and mind, there is no room for idolatry. It's no wonder He made loving Him the first and greatest commandment!

Jesus replied: "'Love the Lord your God with all your heart and with all your soul and with all your mind.' This is the first and greatest commandment.

Matthew 22:37-38

HIS POWER IN OUR WEAKNESS

When we can admit in this self-saturated age that we are not enough on our own, His grace covers our limitations, flaws, and weaknesses so that His power can work through us to purify us and bring Him glory. This is especially evident when we go through hardships and difficulties.

God gave the Apostle Paul plenty to keep him humble throughout his life so he would know he was never enough on his own without God:

Each time he said, "My grace is all you need. My power works best in weakness."
So now I am glad to boast about my weaknesses, so that the power of Christ can
work through me. That's why I take pleasure in my weaknesses, and in the insults,

hardships, persecutions, and troubles that I suffer for Christ. For when I am weak, then I am strong.

2 Corinthians 12:9-10 NLT

When we are weak in ourselves, we become strong in God's grace which keeps us relying on Him for our strength. It is His power that is made perfect in our weakness. God's design is to allow others to see His power in us when He gives us the strength to endure and to even express joy during difficult times.

What hardship have you experienced in your life where God gave you the strength you needed to get through it?

There is no need to ever base your self-worth on what other people tell you about yourself. When you receive God's love and grace, you will find your true self-worth in Him.

No matter how hard you strive, you can never be "enough" on your own. But because Jesus paid the highest price for you, sees you as pure and righteous, and loves you unconditionally despite your limitations, flaws, and weaknesses, your self-worth is secure. There is nothing more valuable than that. You can rest in Him knowing He is more than enough.

THE GIFT OF PURITY FOR A RADIANT LIFE

Through Jesus' unblemished sacrifice on the cross, He has made it possible for you to be spotless, forgiven of all your sin. It is the gracious gift of purity, offered so you can live a radiant life as a new creation here on earth and into eternity.

Dear Heavenly Father,

Thank You for the gift of purity through the sacrifice of Your Son, Jesus Christ, who died on the cross for me and was raised from the dead. I admit that I am a sinner and need Your forgiveness. I am sorry for everything I have done that has not been honoring to You. Please forgive me of all my sin. I accept You as my personal Savior and invite You to be Lord of my life. Thank You for making me pure and unblemished in Your sight and for writing my name in the Lamb's book of life so I will be able to spend eternity with You.

Please give me a spirit of discernment so I will make decisions that please and honor You from now on. I admit I am not enough on my own and need You to be my strength in my weakness. Reveal any idols which may have crept into my heart that I have elevated above You. Transform me to desire to place You above all else so I can love You with all of my heart, soul, and mind. Thank you for loving me.

In Jesus' name,

Amen

TAKE ACTION

If you prayed to receive Jesus Christ as your personal Savior, you are forever saved from your sin and will spend eternity with Him in heaven! Your name has been permanently written in the Lamb's book of life. This is a serious decision, so be sure to tell someone about it and share your good news!

What major decision are you being faced with right now? Take time each day to read God's Word. His principles will be etched on your heart and bonded to your mind to help you make decisions with a spirit of discernment as you come to know Him more intimately.

Ask God for discernment to make the right decisions that honor Him and then journal the direction God is giving you. You will know it comes from Him if it does not contradict Scripture and completely lines up with everything written in His Word. When you make decisions that please Him you will radiantly shine, reflecting Christ in all you do.

LESSON SEVEN

JULY'S BIRTHSTONE: RUBY
The Gift of Wisdom

LESSON SEVEN
July's Birthstone: Ruby - The Gift of Wisdom

KEY VERSE FOR A RADIANT LIFE

For wisdom is far more valuable than rubies. Nothing you desire can compare with it.
Proverbs 8:11 NLT

THE WEALTH OF WISDOM

There was a time in history when women were the most prominent workforce in America. With the men off to fight World War II, women were called to take their place, especially on the production lines to increase the manufacturing of war materials.

After the war was over, most women were let go and returned home as their jobs belonged to the men. With little to buy during the war, these women had saved much of their wages, using their money for the down payment on a house and other sizable expenses to help launch the prosperity of the 1950s.

Many women desired to continue making an income but work from home. This created a whole new industry. Companies like Tupperware and Mary Kay Cosmetics gave women the opportunity to work part-time and sell their products through home parties. Other companies such as Avon and Sara Coventry also used this marketing method for selling their jewelry.

During one of my pursuits to find vintage costume jewelry for repurposing, I found a beautiful pair of ruby red clip earrings from the 1960s era. The stamp on the back was Judy Lee, a trademark used by Blanche-Ette, Inc. which I later discovered also used the home party marketing method during that time and was quite successful.

When I got home, I repurposed my fabulous find into a couple of striking red rings. These red rhinestones remind me of July's traditional birthstone, ruby.

JULY'S BIRTHSTONE

Ruby is a variety of the rock-forming mineral corundum. It is classified as a precious gemstone that varies in color from pink to blood-red. The color is due to the element chromium. Rubies are rare because of the presence of silica or iron, commonly found in the earth's crust which prevents the formation of a ruby.

All natural rubies have imperfections and color impurities. Most are treated in some way to improve the quality with heat treatment as the most common.

Rubies have been mined in several countries including Columbia, Thailand, India, and Japan. A few rubies have also been found in the U.S. in Montana, Wyoming, and the Carolinas.

KING OF JEWELS

The name *ruby* comes from the Latin word *ruber* which means "red." In Sanskrit, ruby is *ratnaraj* meaning "king of jewels." Ruby is considered one of the four precious stones including sapphire, emerald, and diamond.

Ruby is incredibly valuable and can command the highest price per carat of any colored stone. The most valuable shade of red is called *blood-red* or *pigeon blood*. In 2015, a new record was set at an auction for a colored gemstone when a 25.59-carat ruby ring sold for $32.4 million!

As valuable as it is, God values wisdom even more as we can read about in the book of Proverbs:

For wisdom is far more valuable than rubies. Nothing you desire can compare with it.

Proverbs 8:11 NLT

Blessed are those who find wisdom, those who gain understanding, for she is more profitable than silver and yields better returns than gold. She is more precious than rubies; nothing you desire can compare with her. Long life is in her right hand; in her left hand are riches and honor.

Proverbs 3:13-16

THE VALUE OF WISDOM

Job, a wealthy and godly man, knew the incredible value of wisdom even with all of his earthly riches. More importantly, he also knew where to find it…

"But do people know where to find wisdom? Where can they find understanding? No one knows where to find it, for it is not found among the living.

'It is not here,' says the ocean. 'Nor is it here,' says the sea. It cannot be bought with gold. It cannot be purchased with silver.

It's worth more than all the gold of Ophir, greater than precious onyx or lapis lazuli. Wisdom is more valuable than gold and crystal. It cannot be purchased with jewels mounted in fine gold. Coral and jasper are worthless in trying to get it. The price of wisdom is far above rubies. Precious peridot from Ethiopia cannot be exchanged for it. It's worth more than the purest gold.

"But do people know where to find wisdom? Where can they find understanding? It is hidden from the eyes of all humanity. Even the sharp-eyed birds in the sky cannot discover it.

Destruction and Death say, 'We've heard only rumors of where wisdom can be found.'

"God alone understands the way to wisdom; he knows where it can be found, for he looks throughout the whole earth and sees everything under the heavens. He decided how hard the winds should blow and how much rain should fall. He made the laws for the rain and laid out a path for the lightning.

Then he saw wisdom and evaluated it. He set it in place and examined it thoroughly. And this is what he says to all humanity: 'The fear of the Lord is true wisdom; to forsake evil is real understanding.'"

Job 28:12-28 NLT

THE FEAR OF THE LORD

So there you have it! Wisdom is found in God alone. Because God is all-powerful and all-knowing, we fear Him meaning we stand in awe of Him.

The fear of the Lord begins when we see our Creator worthy of glory and honor. We acknowledge Him as Lord of our lives, have a sincere commitment to obey

Him, and a desire for Him to be involved in the decisions we make by asking Him for wisdom.

"Worthy are you, our Lord and God, to receive glory and honor and power, for you created all things, and by your will they existed and were created."

Revelation 4:11 ESV

Now, we will never have the kind of wisdom to understand all of the mysteries of God while we are here on earth. That is for God to know and keep secret until those mysteries are revealed to us one day in our eternal Home with Him. Truly something we can look forward to!

As Job explains in great detail how God orchestrated everything in nature to work in harmony, those are examples of the things in this life that we will never fully understand.

What is a particular mystery of God that you would like to ask Him about when you are living in your eternal Home with Him?

God also knows how to orchestrate everything in our lives to work in perfect harmony. He knows it all from beginning to end. There is nothing hidden from Him whether it be past, present, or future. What a huge risk we are taking when we do not seek His counsel first!

Having God's wisdom protects us from making unwise decisions that can cause pain and suffering which could have easily been avoided if we had simply asked Him for wisdom.

When have you experienced God's wisdom protecting you from making an unwise decision?

God's wisdom is a gift that we cannot earn, purchase, or obtain in any way on our own. He graciously gives it to us anytime we ask.

If any of you lacks wisdom, you should ask God, who gives generously to all without finding fault, and it will be given to you.

James 1:5

GOD'S GIFT TO US

We find wisdom by regularly reading, studying, and meditating on God's Word. This is how God speaks to us. He has graciously gifted us with His instruction book for our lives so we will have everything we need to know to live a life that is pleasing and honoring to Him. That is the only way we can truly prosper and succeed in any of our efforts.

Study this Book of Instruction continually. Meditate on it day and night so you will be sure to obey everything written in it. Only then will you prosper and succeed in all you do.

Joshua 1:8 NLT

ETERNAL RICHES

Rubies have an earthly value that only lasts for a short time, but wisdom has a heavenly value which will last for eternity. Perhaps you have been blessed with earthly, temporal wealth, but how rich is your relationship with God?

Do you see your Creator worthy of glory and honor? Do you acknowledge Him as Lord of your life? Are you fully committed to obeying Him? If so, you have the fear of the Lord and because of it, the wealth of wisdom to give you a life filled with the richness of His incredible blessings that reach into eternity.

Jesus told a parable of the rich fool who was completely self-focused on earthly pleasures and left God out of the picture by not asking Him for wisdom when he was faced with making a major decision:

Then he told them a story: "A rich man had a fertile farm that produced fine crops. He said to himself, 'What should I do? I don't have room for all my crops.' Then he said, 'I know! I'll tear down my barns and build bigger ones.

Then I'll have room enough to store all my wheat and other goods. And I'll sit back and say to myself, "My friend, you have enough stored away for years to come. Now take it easy! Eat, drink, and be merry!"'

"But God said to him, 'You fool! You will die this very night. Then who will get everything you worked for?'

"Yes, a person is a fool to store up earthly wealth but not have a rich relationship with God."

Luke 12:16-21 NLT

Are you investing more of your time in striving for earthly wealth rather than in your relationship with God? _____ If so, what are some things you can do to invest more time in your relationship with God?

The riches of this life are fleeting. When you include God in your decisions by asking Him for wisdom, your work on earth has eternal significance. Long life, riches, and honor are a few of the blessings you will receive in your heavenly Home…a Home that will be filled with eternal treasures far more valuable than even the finest rubies.

NUMBER YOUR DAYS FOR A HEART OF WISDOM

Tick tock, tick tock. As I'm typing away on my computer, I glance at the clock on the wall. A feeling of urgency wells up inside of me as the second hand steadily moves around in perfect rhythm, mercilessly counting down my finite heartbeats.

Every second we're given has been predetermined by God. Every breath we take is a gift. As we go about our busy lives, we often forget about the brevity of life – how short our time here on earth really is.

Moses must have given that some deep thought as he prayed this prayer:

Teach us to number our days, that we may gain a heart of wisdom.

Psalm 90:12

Without giving our limited time on earth much thought, we can easily get swept up in the insignificant things of life that have no eternal value. And we end up wasting time. Lots of time. Watching hours and hours of television, scrolling endlessly through social media, and shopping for more stuff that we don't need are a few of the typical ways we waste our precious time.

So what exactly does it mean to number our days?

What it does *not* mean is counting how many days we've lived so far or trying to figure out how many we have left. What it *does* mean is being aware of the shortness of life and having a desire to live each day to the fullest for God's purposes and for His glory. It means using our time wisely.

ETERNITY-FOCUSED PURPOSE

Recognizing the value of time is absolutely essential if you are to gain a heart of wisdom. It is then that you will seek to make the most out of your time on earth. There are opportunities all around you offering ways for you to make good use of your time, filling each day with eternity-focused purpose. But these opportunities don't last forever. There is usually a very brief window of time to seize them.

God provides you with everything you need, from unique talents and gifts to a variety of resources to be shared with others, so you can spend your time wisely on that which has eternal value.

The world's ideas about what is valuable is not transferable to eternity such as wealth, possessions, comfort, status, and power. Only God and people have eternal value, so the way we spend our time should be motivated by loving God and people.

Look around to see where you might be able to help someone. There are opportunities to meet needs everywhere you go. You just have to open your eyes and be willing to give of your time. Serving others has eternal value. You are demonstrating God's love as you selflessly give of your time and energy.

Write about a time when you saw a need and helped out by serving:

I recently became reacquainted with an old friend I met in junior high when I was living in California. We lost touch and it had been nearly 30 years since we'd spoken. Carol still had the same laugh and we talked on the phone for hours every Sunday, reminiscing and chatting about life during the past three decades. Every phone call ended with Carol asking to pray for me even though she was very ill. She loved to pray!

Sadly, she was battling stage four breast cancer and had very little energy to do the things most of us often take advantage of being able to do. Things like brushing her teeth, washing her hair, preparing food, or tidying up her house.

During a particularly hard day, a friend of hers came over to bring her some food since she could no longer drive to go to the grocery store. Her friend took a look around and said, "These dirty floors are really bothering me. Let me clean them for you!"

Carol was so thrilled because they had been bothering her too, but there was nothing she could do about it since she had no energy for a monumental task like that. Her friend then began to vacuum and mop all of the floors in the house till they were sparkling.

The opportunity was there and she acted on it to meet a need. She opened her eyes to see it and was willing to spend her time and energy in a way that showed so much love to her friend. Definitely time well spent with eternal value!

It was a very brief window of time for her friend to seize that opportunity to serve as Carol lost her battle to breast cancer just a few weeks later, passing from this life immediately into the loving arms of Jesus.

LIVE WITH ETERNITY IN MIND

If you are a follower of Christ, you cannot live foolishly and stay close to Him at the same time. When you repeatedly ignore the opportunities God places in front of you to serve Him, you will slowly be drawn away from Him as you live more and more for yourself and your own selfish desires. Life will soon become full of too-lates. Those opportunities may never return.

When you number your days, however, you are cautious and careful with how you spend your time because you have a heart of wisdom. A heart that pursues opportunities with eternal impact will make you more like Christ, radiant in the image of God.

So be careful how you live. Don't live like fools, but like those who are wise. Make the most of every opportunity in these evil days.

Ephesians 5:15-16 NLT

Living without keeping eternity in mind is foolish. Life is short. After this life, you will come face-to-face with eternity where you will be forever with God or forever separated from Him. You may come to the end of your life more quickly than you think.

THE GOOD NEWS

The Apostle Peter reminds us of the shortness of our lives:

As the Scriptures say, "People are like grass; their beauty is like a flower in the field. The grass withers and the flower fades. But the word of the Lord remains forever." And that word is the Good News that was preached to you.

1 Peter 1:24-25 NLT

The Good News is that you don't have to be separated from God forever. When you believe in Jesus Christ as your Savior and repent of your sin, you are admitting that you can't save yourself. Instead, you are relying on Him to save you.

The Good News is that He died for you and rose from the dead. What this means is that even though you are a sinner, you can be made righteous, completely cleansed inside from all of your sin so you can share in an eternal inheritance with Him. That is incredibly good news!

Be ready for eternity by choosing Jesus to be your Savior before the last tick of the clock, your final heartbeat.

THE GIFT OF WISDOM FOR A RADIANT LIFE

Number your days, spending your time on what matters for eternity. Fear the Lord by pursuing the opportunities God gives you to bring Him glory because He is worthy. Study God's Word continually so that you may gain a heart of wisdom, an incredible gift for a radiant life.

Dear Heavenly Father,

Thank You for the gift of wisdom. I am so grateful You are willing to give it generously whenever I ask for it. I acknowledge You as Lord of my life, worthy of all glory and honor. Please help me to remember my time on earth is limited so I will use what is left of it wisely, taking advantage of the windows of opportunity You have given me to serve others. Thank You so much for giving me Your instruction book filled with Your wisdom.

In Jesus' name,

Amen

TAKE ACTION

At the end of each day this week, journal how you spent your time. How could you have used your time more wisely? Replace time-wasters with the opportunities God gives you that will make an eternal impact.

Write down any opportunities He shows you to serve others and be sure to act on them when they come up. Take time to read, study, and meditate on God's Word daily to fill your mind with godly wisdom for a life that glorifies Him.

JOURNAL

LESSON EIGHT

AUGUST'S BIRTHSTONE: PERIDOT
The Gift of Intimacy

LESSON EIGHT

August's Birthstone: Peridot - The Gift of Intimacy

KEY VERSE FOR A RADIANT LIFE

O LORD, You have searched me and known me. You know when I sit down and when I rise up; You understand my thought from afar. You scrutinize my path and my lying down, and are intimately acquainted with all my ways.

Psalm 139:1-3 NASB

A RICH RELATIONSHIP WITH GOD

It was the weekend of the International Gem and Jewelry Show. I always look forward to it with great anticipation. Vendors from all over the world gather twice a year in Dallas to display and sell their raw or polished gemstones as well as their stunning jewelry designs.

I am absolutely fascinated with these brilliant, colorful stones that naturally form in the earth's crust or a bit deeper in molten rock.

While I was there visiting with a vendor from India, he showed me gemstones in every color which had been made into beads. It was right then that I had the idea to create birthstone necklaces.

By the end of my shopping day, I was able to purchase gemstone beads representing every month's traditional birthstone (except diamond which I substituted with crystal quartz) to make these necklaces. I then found delicate, 24k gold overlay and rhodium plated chain along with pavé CZ beads for a little added sparkle.

After adding these new necklace designs to my website, God put it on my heart to donate a portion of the sale of each necklace to the non-profit organization Human Coalition to help with their mission of protecting pre-born babies in the womb, rescuing them from abortion. What a great reminder these birthstone necklaces were to me of the precious gift of life!

AUGUST'S BIRTHSTONE

One of the gemstones I used to make these necklaces is August's traditional birthstone peridot.

Peridot, pronounced *pair-uh-doe*, is derived from the Greek word *peridona* meaning "to give richness." It is the gem-quality variety of olivine which is actually quite rare and one of the few gemstones that occurs in only one color, an olive green. The intensity of the color depends upon the amount of iron present. The more intense the color, the greater the value.

Most peridot today is mined by Native Americans in Arizona on the San Carlos Reservation. Other states where it can found include Arkansas, Hawaii, Nevada, and New Mexico. It is also mined in Australia, Myanmar, China, and Sri Lanka.

In 1994, a new deposit of peridot was discovered in Pakistan and was among the finest peridot that has ever been seen.

I found a piece of olivine vintage costume jewelry in my collection from the 1960s era that sparkles so brightly with its rich peridot rhinestones in both round and marquise shapes.

THE RICHES OF GOD'S GRACE

While we are still living here on earth in our temporary home, God greatly desires to have a relationship with us. Why? Because He loves us so much and wants to be included in our daily lives so He can give us the guidance we need to stay on His perfect path - the path that will bring the most blessing to our lives because He wants the very best for us.

The characteristics of peridot remind me so much of the way our relationship works with God. Just as the intensity of the color depends upon the amount of iron in the gemstone, the intensity of our relationship with God depends upon how much time we spend with Him by taking our requests to Him in prayer, asking Him for wisdom and discernment, and listening to Him when He speaks to us while reading His Word.

The more intense the color of peridot, the greater the value. The more intense or strong our relationship is with God, the greater we value it.

Think about your relationship with a very dear friend. You tend to value it much more than you would an acquaintance because of the personal closeness you feel with them. They are involved in your life, you talk to them often, you ask them for advice, and share intimate details about your life with them. And they reciprocate by listening well and also sharing deeply with you.

The meaning of peridot, "to give richness," is comprehensible now when you can imagine it with full-color intensity. When you become a follower of Christ, His grace redeems you, delivering you from the bondage of your deepest, darkest sin so He could provide richness and radiance to your life through the intensity of His love for you.

In him we have redemption through his blood, the forgiveness of sins, in accordance with the riches of God's grace that he lavished on us.

Ephesians 1:7-8a

What a gift to be given the opportunity to have a rich relationship with God…one that starts here on earth and continues in His magnificent kingdom all through eternity!

FULLY KNOWN AND DEEPLY LOVED

How well do you know yourself? If you were to be completely honest, you probably don't know yourself as well as you think you do.

Human beings are complex and continually changing. I have noticed multiple changes in myself over the years. One example is my taste in home decor. It has gone from everything white and glass with a light, contemporary look to dark, heavy wood and iron. In the last couple of years, my decorating taste changed again to everything bright, colorful, and modern!

On a deeper level, changes have taken place with whom I consider my closest friends. Positive and negative life experiences with people, the passing of time, and moving often during my growing up years have all impacted those I choose to welcome into my inner circle.

I have also seen my very own identity change in the way I define myself. I've noticed I tend to put a lot of emphasis on who I am based on what interests I am most passionate about at the moment. Right now, I define myself as a blogger, book writer, jewelry designer, and water fitness enthusiast.

How would you define who you are based on your interests?

More importantly, who are you on the inside? That is also continually changing. One of the greatest longings of the human soul is to be able to fully know and understand ourselves.

Some of the questions you might ask yourself are:

Why do I do what I do? What drives me? What are my motives? What are my deepest wounds and why do they hurt me so much?

CREATED TO BE FULLY KNOWN

The only way toward complete self-understanding is by having a relationship with God. He knows everything about you. There is no one else who can know you fully and completely like He does. In His perfect timing, He will reveal the deepest parts of who you are so He can do His work in you, shaping you to become more like Him.

O LORD, You have searched me and known me. You know when I sit down and when I rise up; You understand my thought from afar. You scrutinize my path and my lying down, and are intimately acquainted with all my ways. Even before there is a word on my tongue, behold, O LORD, You know it all.

Psalm 139:1-4 NASB

You were created to be fully known. Even though God already knows everything about you, He desires for you to be open and vulnerable so you can enjoy a fulfilling, rich relationship with Him and receive the total extent of His deep love for you. When you are fully known, you can then discover who you are. It also intensifies your need for God as you realize your greatest weaknesses.

What is something that God has shown you about yourself through spending time with Him?

In this world, the way we are perceived is valued far above reality. Through our social media posts and how we present ourselves so flawless and perfectly polished to others, we are constantly trying to create an image covering up who we really are.

Why do we do this? To avoid rejection. But the more we fake it, the less we are truly loved. If someone loves an image of yourself that you have created, you cannot actually receive that love because it isn't real. To be fully known is to be deeply loved.

This is a great explanation from Timothy Keller's book *The Meaning of Marriage*:

> To be loved but not known is comforting but superficial. To be known and not loved is our greatest fear. But to be fully known and truly loved is, well, a lot like being loved by God. It is what we need more than anything. It liberates us from pretense, humbles us out of our self-righteousness, and fortifies us for any difficulty life can throw at us.

Think about a relationship in your life in which you both deeply love each other. Most likely, it took quite awhile to feel that kind of love for one another.

Relationships take time and effort to get to a place where you feel safe and free to share your heart. To have a real relationship, you cannot just talk about the surface stuff (like your taste in home decor). At some point, your conversations have to go much deeper so you can truly know and understand each other. Once you get to that level, you can then experience a genuine love.

Who is someone you feel truly knows and understands you?

As strong as your love may be, however, it is often conditional. I've had friends in the past with whom I have had a very close bond. I would've thought nothing could ever tear our friendship apart. But if something happens along the way to weaken that bond such as breaking my trust, my love for them and our friendship is no longer the same.

NO MATTER WHAT

God's love is much different. It is not conditional or based on anything that you do or don't do, good or bad. To experience the depths of His love is to understand that you are loved no matter what. It doesn't matter if you are addicted to drugs or alcohol, cheated on your spouse, had an abortion, committed a crime, or even hate God. You can never be unlovable! You are totally forgiven and nothing can ever take away His love for you.

And may you have the power to understand, as all God's people should, how wide, how long, how high, and how deep his love is. May you experience the love of Christ, though it is too great to understand fully. Then you will be made complete with all the fullness of life and power that comes from God.

Ephesians 3:18-19 NLT

God is very patient. He will wait as long as it takes for you to share your heart with Him without reservation. He greatly desires a close, intimate relationship with you.

God already knows all the secrets of your life, so there is nothing to hide. Know that when you do share your heart, He will never reject you. Trust that He is a good Father who simply wants to love you deeply.

Yes, you are complex and continually changing. Your tastes change, your friendships change, and who you are based on your passions of the moment goes through change.

But God's love for you never changes. And who you are in Him has nothing to do with how you or anyone else defines you. When you become a follower of Christ, He gives you a brand new identity.

You are completely secure in God's love. Know that you can come boldly before Him, unpolished, with all of your flaws exposed. It is then that He can begin to shape you into the beautiful creation He made you to be…fully known and deeply loved.

SEEKING GOD'S PRESENCE

If I was to describe myself, one of the first words that pops into my mind is *minimalist*. When it comes to my home, I do not like clutter, too many nicknacks, or anything lying around out of place that is not being used. I do like lots of space, cleanliness, and a few things I value around me that may not function for any other reason than to bring a smile to my face when I see them.

Even as a minimalist, my space can begin to feel cluttered if I don't keep up with putting things back where they belong or stay on top of being organized with all the little things that tend to pile up.

I have noticed I can get easily distracted and am not able to focus very well with clutter. So, I have made it a habit to try to make order of any "chaos" around me by putting everything back in its proper place before I begin anything that requires deep concentration. I know that to have order is to have peace for my mind and spirit.

CENTERED ON ORDER

I began thinking about how much the universe is associated with what I crave… order. God's divine plan was centered on order when He created it.

For example, the distance of the moon from the earth is 240,000 miles. If it was only 50,000 miles, the gravitational pull from the moon would be so strong that the ocean tides would fully submerge the earth's surface twice every day!

There was no room for chaos of any kind for the universe to be able to function in the exact and precise way it did then and still does today – in perfect order.

Sir Isaac Newton (1643 - 1727) is widely recognized as one of the most influential scientists of all time. He discovered the theory of gravity. As he worked hard to uncover the laws about the "order" of the universe, he began to see God as the masterful Creator whose existence could not be denied with the splendor of creation and its precision that followed an orderly pattern and plan:

> "This most beautiful system of the sun, planets, and comets could only proceed from the counsel and dominion of an intelligent Being. This Being governs all things, not as the soul of the world, but as Lord over all; and on account of his dominion he is wont to be called "Lord God" or "Universal Ruler." The Supreme God is a Being eternal, infinite, [and] absolutely perfect."

Newton's belief lines up beautifully with what Scripture tell us about creation and order:

Thus says the LORD, who gives the sun for light by day and the fixed order of the moon and the stars for light by night, who stirs up the sea so that its waves roar – the LORD of hosts is his name:

Jeremiah 31:35 ESV

After reading this verse, how would you describe God?

SEEK GOD'S PRESENCE CONTINUALLY

When it comes to our lives, we all want order. We want peace. No one desires to live in constant chaos. We want to know that we are on the right path headed in the direction that will provide the least amount of chaos for us.

God gives us plenty of freedom when it comes to making choices – from which job to take, to what part of the world to live in, who to marry, and on it goes.

There can be good that comes from several of those choices set before us. But the best way to determine God's best and to keep from making destructive decisions that lead to chaos is to have a relationship with Him. A relationship where we seek God continually and with all of our heart.

What does it mean to seek God?

To seek God means to seek His presence. *Presence* is the Hebrew word used in the Old Testament for "face." A person's face reveals so much about their character. Emotions and feelings are expressed on a person's face. You recognize someone by seeing their face. It represents who they are.

When you seek God's face, you are desiring to know His character and be in His presence more than anything else. Your mind and heart are fully focused on Him. The more you seek to be in His presence, the more your character and desires will begin to align with His. You will know Him intimately, understand how much He loves you, and have enough faith to fully trust Him.

There will be no reason to ever worry or be filled with anxiety about making the right choices. When you are seeking His presence, He is continually guiding you on the path that gives your life a beautiful sense of order.

Seek the LORD and his strength; seek his presence continually!

1 Chronicles 16:11 ESV

So how do we seek God's presence? His presence is found in who He is, as our Creator and as our Companion.

GOD IS OUR CREATOR

God's glory is all around us. We can look up into the expansive heavens or take in the colorful flowers, unusual wildlife, towering trees, majestic mountains, or the powerful ocean to see His glory. We can seek Him as the Master Creator and praise Him for the magnificent way He displays His glory in His creation.

The heavens declare the glory of God, and the sky above proclaims his handiwork.

Psalm 19:1 ESV

Have you ever been to a place where God's majesty was clearly evident to you in nature? _____ If so, where? _____

How would you describe it?

Michael and I took a trip to Lake Tahoe several years ago and everywhere my eye traveled, I was in awe! The glory of God was so evident in the beauty of nature surrounding us. When I look back at this photo taken of us there, I feel so insignificant. I am this tiny dot surrounded by the majesty of God's creation!

Reading Psalm 139, however, gives me the assurance that I am actually quite significant in God's eyes. He spent time creating me, knitting me together in my mother's womb. I am a complex masterpiece!

Read these verses from Psalm 139 out loud to God, praising Him for His wonderful works in the way He made you:

For you created my inmost being; you knit me together in my mother's womb. I praise you because I am fearfully and wonderfully made; your works are wonderful, I know that full well.

Psalm 139:13-14

There is an order to your make-up as all of the parts of your body must work together, each with their own God-given job, yet dependent on the other parts so they can function properly and precisely.

To have life, there must be specific chemistry. God created the laws of chemistry with perfection and order so that life would be possible. God's glory is displayed in you just as it is in nature when you use the unique abilities God has given you. When you are seeking His presence, He will continually show you, time after time, exactly how you can use your abilities for His glory. He will provide those perfect opportunities for you.

God has given us His Word to reveal who He is. We are seeking His presence when we spend time reading it. Throughout the Bible, we discover how much He loves us. We learn about His attributes that make up His character such as being a personal God who deeply desires a rich relationship with us to be our faithful Companion.

We also learn about His laws which lead us to the path of life – the path that is filled with joy, godly pleasures, order, and peace!

You make known to me the path of life; in your presence there is fullness of joy; at your right hand are pleasures forevermore.

Psalm 16:11 ESV

If you have difficulty making it a priority to spend time with God, ask Him to give you an insatiable desire for reading His Word so you can get to know Him deeply. Relationships take time and commitment!

I like to read my Bible in the morning, letting the first voice I hear be God's voice. I start my day being reminded of His unfailing love for me. He gives me direction with an eternal perspective on my day's plans and the decisions that I will face.

Let the morning bring me word of your unfailing love, for I have put my trust in you. Show me the way I should go, for to you I entrust my life.

Psalm 143:8

Another advantage to reading God's Word in the morning is that certain passages will stick with me, encouraging me all throughout the day. Memorize verses that speak to you as you read so they will easily come to mind whenever you need them, helping you continually seek the presence of God.

At times, you may find it difficult to sense God's presence with all of the "noise" going on around you – the constant busyness of life. It can easily drown out His voice as He is trying to speak to your heart.

Sadly, we are often too busy and too self-absorbed to truly seek Him as we should. We make everything but God a priority. It doesn't take long before our lives are filled with disorder and chaos.

That is why He tells us to seek His presence continually. Only then can we experience peace which is the absence of chaos. It is a daily, conscious choice to include Him as our Companion in our thoughts and activities throughout the day. And it is also a conscious choice to steer clear of those things that dull us spiritually which can keep us from desiring to seek Him.

Establish my footsteps in Your word, and do not let any iniquity have dominion over me.

Psalm 119:133 NASB

What kinds of things have you found in your life that dull you spiritually?

God is a God of order. Just as He has specific laws of precision and order for the moon and stars to stay on their celestial path, how much more does He desire to provide precision that follows an orderly pattern and plan for you who He created and deeply loves! All that is required of you is to seek His presence and He will graciously make known to you the path of life.

THE GIFT OF INTIMACY FOR A RADIANT LIFE

The gift of intimacy with God provides a radiant life filled with the richness in your relationship with Him, redemption through His grace, unconditional love, and perfect order when you seek His presence.

Dear Heavenly Father,

Thank You for the gift of intimacy. I am so grateful to be fully known and deeply loved by You, my Creator. Please deepen my desire to seek Your presence for a rich relationship with You now and into eternity. Thank You for showing me the path of life and how I can experience Your peace, guidance, and fullness of joy when I am in Your presence.

In Jesus' name,

Amen

TAKE ACTION

Build the intensity of your relationship with God by seeking His presence. Spend quality time with Him as you read His Word to hear His voice and ask for His guidance and wisdom as you share the intimate details of your life with Him. If you struggle being open and vulnerable with God, ask Him to help you feel safe and secure in His love for you so you can experience a close relationship with Him.

JOURNAL

LESSON NINE

SEPTEMBER'S BIRTHSTONE: SAPPHIRE
The Gift of Victory

LESSON NINE
September's Birthstone: Sapphire - The Gift of Victory

KEY VERSE FOR A RADIANT LIFE

But thanks be to God, who gives us the victory through our Lord Jesus Christ.

1 Corinthians 15:57 ESV

SHAPED THROUGH FRICTION FOR VICTORY

It was 1939. The Great Depression had finally ended and fashion magazines were beginning to be printed in color, giving clothing and jewelry a bright, cheerful look. This greatly helped to boost morale during these troublesome times.

Hollywood actresses wore eye-catching, colorful costume jewelry on-screen and in the magazines. Their sparkly jewelry made quite a statement. It was often created with rhinestones to look like gemstones which gave the illusion of wealth and prosperity.

Women of this era wanted that glamorous look without the high price tag, so these designs were replicated into jewelry that was affordable for women of all social classes. It was then sold at five and dime stores like Woolworth's and Kresge's. It did not take long before costume jewelry became extremely fashionable and popular.

As a collector of vintage costume jewelry, I have come across some of the most gorgeous rhinestone pieces that could easily be mistaken for authentic gemstones. This is one I acquired that looks like it was made with costly sapphires:

SEPTEMBER'S BIRTHSTONE

Sapphire is September's traditional birthstone. The name sapphire comes from the Latin word *saphirus* and the Greek word *sapheiros*, both meaning "blue." This is the color for which sapphire is most known.

Sapphire is considered one of the four precious gemstones which also include diamond, ruby, and emerald. It is a variety of the rock-forming mineral corundum which typically contains traces of elements such as iron, magnesium, chromium, and titanium.

Although sapphire is usually recognized for its rich blue color, these elements allow for sapphire to be found in other colors as well such as yellow, purple, pink, orange, and green. These are called "fancy" sapphires.

Pink sapphires deepen in color the more chromium they have in them which increases the value. If it deepens too much, it becomes red which classifies it as a ruby, one of the most valuable gemstones. If it has two or more colors, it is called a "parti-colored" sapphire commonly found in Australia.

Interestingly, sapphires cannot be created synthetically. They only occur naturally. Huge sapphire deposits are located in countries such as Thailand, Sri Lanka, Burma, Madagascar, and in North America in the state of Montana.

MOHS HARDNESS SCALE

In 1812, a German geologist and mineralogist named Friedrich Mohs developed a hardness scale for minerals so that a mineral of unknown hardness could be tested against a group of 10 index minerals to see where it would rank.

The test compared the resistance of a mineral to being scratched. He selected 10 minerals that ranged from very soft (talc) to very hard (diamond) and rated them on a scale from one to ten.

The Mohs Hardness Scale has been widely used throughout the world for over 200 years:

Mohs Hardness Scale	
Mineral	Hardness
Talc	1
Gypsum	2
Calcite	3
Fluorite	4
Apatite	5
Ortoclase	6
Quartz	7
Topaz	8
Corundum	9
Diamond	10

CORUNDUM AS AN ABRASIVE

As you can see from the scale, corundum is an exceptionally hard material falling just below the hardness of diamond. Because sapphire is a variety of corundum, it's easy to cut without having it crumble. It can also put up with a lot of wear, making it a desirable gemstone to use in a jewelry setting.

The incredible hardness of corundum makes it especially useful as an abrasive, a material that is used to shape a softer material by wearing part of it away through friction. Corundum is crushed and processed to remove its impurities and then made into granules and powders which are used in tools such as polishing compounds, sandpapers, and grinding wheels.

One of the most common uses for natural corundum with which most of us are familiar is an emery board or nail file. Abrasive papers are glued to a thin piece of cardboard and then used as a tool to grind down and shape the edges of fingernails.

Emery boards got their name during the 1800s when crushed emery stone, very rich in corundum, was used as the abrasive. Today's emery boards are only made with synthetic corundum but are often still sold as "emery boards."

LIFE IS FULL OF ABRASIVES

As we go through life, we all experience different kinds of abrasives. They come in the form of trials, afflictions, heartaches, illness, disappointments, difficulties, trauma, grief, shame, and guilt, just to name a few.

Some abrasives may be no fault of our own such as having a loved one taken from us too early, suffering from a long-term illness, or not being married by the age we had set for ourselves to have walked down the aisle with that perfect partner.

Others, however, are a direct result of the choices we make that do not honor God. The friction that takes place from each of these kinds of abrasives shapes us in a unique way and often times for a new purpose in life. No matter what the reason for the abrasive, God can use it to shape us so we reflect His character.

Often, our first reaction to an abrasive is anger, bitterness, or perhaps even feelings of hopelessness. Over time, we can get stuck in these thought patterns that are incredibly damaging to our heart, mind, and spirit. They keep us from being able to see how God can find beauty in our difficult circumstance while making us stronger in our faith.

What are some of the difficult abrasives you've gone through in life?

RELEASING THOUGHT PATTERNS OF BONDAGE

Michael and I had just come back from a week of vacationing in Asheville, North Carolina. I swam nearly every morning in the beautiful, indoor pool of our hotel.

On one side of the pool was a wall that was made of all glass. When I would arrive early in the morning and take a look outside, there was nothing to see but a heavy mist hiding everything behind it. But by the time I was just about finished swimming, the mist would begin to clear and I could then see the beautiful Blue Ridge Mountains dotted with thousands of pine trees in the distance. It was an incredible scenic view that I never would have known existed unless the mist lifted.

Think of your anger, bitterness, or hopelessness as that dense mist hiding the beauty God is able to find in whatever it is causing friction in your life to lead you to a new purpose and a closer relationship with Him. It is never God's desire for you to get stuck in thought patterns that cause bondage. Only after you let go and release it all to Him will He be able to give you complete freedom and show you His grace by blessing you with victory.

But thanks be to God, who gives us the victory through our Lord Jesus Christ.

1 Corinthians 15:57 ESV

Have you been able to release your thought patterns of bondage that cause friction in your life? _____ If not, what is holding you back?

GROW CLOSER TO GOD THROUGH ABRASIVES

I don't think I have ever heard anyone say, "I grew so much closer to God when everything was going smoothly in my life."

It is usually through the abrasives that you grow closer to God. You begin to give Him more of your attention as you see your need for Him. You cry out to Him for help, relying on Him to get you through the pain of your difficult circumstance. And your faith becomes strengthened as you see Him work in your life for your good.

Have you ever experienced growing closer to God through the abrasives in your life? _____ If so, how?

The Apostle Paul experienced a life full of abrasives, one after the other:

I have worked harder, been put in prison more often, been whipped times without number, and faced death again and again. Five different times the Jewish leaders gave me thirty-nine lashes. Three times I was beaten with rods. Once I was stoned. Three times I was shipwrecked.

Once I spent a whole night and a day adrift at sea. I have traveled on many long journeys. I have faced danger from rivers and from robbers. I have faced danger from my own people, the Jews, as well as from the Gentiles. I have faced danger in the cities, in the deserts, and on the seas. And I have faced danger from men who claim to be believers but are not. I have worked hard and long, enduring many sleepless nights. I have been hungry and thirsty and have often gone without food. I have shivered in the cold, without enough clothing to keep me warm.

2 Corinthians 11:23b-27 NLT

Through each abrasive, Paul became stronger as he learned to see the good that God intended for his life in order for others to see the power of Christ in him:

Each time he said, "My grace is all you need. My power works best in weakness." So now I am glad to boast about my weaknesses, so that the power of Christ can work through me. That's why I take pleasure in my weaknesses, and in the insults, hardships, persecutions, and troubles that I suffer for Christ. For when I am weak, then I am strong.

2 Corinthians 12:9-10 NLT

ABRASIVE CONSEQUENCES

Often times, it is our own choices in life that result in painful, abrasive consequences. These are choices that go against God's Word. When we lose our awareness of God and begin to act as if He does not exist, we suffer from the consequences of making our own choices without His blessing. It is our suffering, however, that reminds us of our need for Him. That suffering is His mercy for us so we will come back to Him.

What choices have you made in life that resulted in painful consequences?

As our Creator, He knows what is best for our lives. When we choose to value what

He values, we mature spiritually and experience His incredible blessings that He can't wait to give to us because He loves us so much!

And God is able to bless you abundantly, so that in all things at all times, having all that you need, you will abound in every good work.

2 Corinthians 9:8

A dear friend of mine made the choice at the age of 18 to have an abortion. Over the years, she began to feel a heavy burden of guilt and shame for terminating her pregnancy. She knew God loved her but could not accept that He fully forgave her.

The turning point for her was when she found out about an after-abortion recovery ministry called Someone Cares, a 12-week study of God's plan for women who have experienced the pain of abortion using a "Forgiven and Set Free" program which helps them to discover freedom, hope, healing, and restoration.

After completing the program, my friend told me she no longer feels stuck in her guilt and shame and has complete freedom to finally move forward and to even help other women with their post-abortion healing journey. Christ has given her victory over her pain which she is now using to glorify Him through her new purpose.

She shared one of her favorite Scripture verses with me which has been a great reminder of God's character and love for her throughout this incredibly abrasive experience:

He has removed our sins as far from us as the east is from the west.

Psalm 103:12 NLT

What an incredible promise God gives to us to experience total freedom and victory through Him!

FRICTION FOR SHAPING

God uses the abrasives in our lives for so many different reasons. Often times, we can look back after enduring a difficult trial and can see how God was able to accomplish something good through it. Here are a few of the ways He uses our sufferings for our good:

- Helps us recognize and remove sinful behaviors from our life

- Strengthens our relationship with Him

- Gives us a reason to depend on His grace

- Increases our wisdom and discernment

- Produces perseverance and character

- Builds our trust and hope in Christ

- Offers freedom and joy

- Allows us to boast of victory for God's glory

Just as corundum is used for grinding and shaping, God uses the friction of life's abrasives to shape us so we can be given a new purpose, reflecting Him with the beauty of freedom through each miraculous victory.

LIVE IN VICTORY WITH THE ARMOR OF GOD

The beginning of each new year that we are given feels hopeful. We anticipate a year filled with sweet memories to be made, exciting adventures to experience, and abundant blessings to enjoy. But there are also the inevitable challenges to face.

At times, these challenges may feel like major battles you are forced to fight. Whether you realize it or not, there are continuous battles going on – spiritual battles – fighting hard for your mind, your heart, and your spirit. They can leave you feeling defeated if you are unprepared for the many fiery arrows that come flying in your direction.

These arrows are coming from Satan, the god of this world, who would love to keep you chained in darkness where you would be unable to experience for yourself or spread to others the Good News of God's plan - His plan for you to be able to live in the light with eternal freedom from sin.

THE PROTECTIVE ARMOR OF GOD

When you become a follower of Christ, He gives you everything you need to fight those spiritual battles…and WIN. You do not have to fear because you have His mighty strength and power to rely on with full protection. This protection is incredibly strong armor which includes a belt, breastplate, shoes, shield, helmet, and sword.

The Apostle Paul writes:

Finally, be strong in the Lord and in his mighty power. Put on the full armor of God so that you can take your stand against the devil's schemes. For our struggle is not against flesh and blood, but against the rulers, against the authorities, against the powers of this dark world and against the spiritual forces of evil in the heavenly realms.

Therefore put on the full armor of God, so that when the day of evil comes, you may be able to stand your ground, and after you have done everything, to stand. Stand firm then, with the belt of truth buckled around your waist, with the breastplate of righteousness in place, and with your feet fitted with the readiness that comes from the gospel of peace. In addition to all this, take up the shield of faith, with which you can extinguish all the flaming arrows of the evil one. Take the helmet of salvation and sword of the Spirit which is the word of God.

Ephesians 6:10-17

We are given everything we need for protection, but notice Paul says that we are to take action by putting on the full armor of God. We cannot just let the armor sit around and get dusty. We have to put it on each day so we can use it!

ARMOR FOR THE BATTLE FOR YOUR MIND: BELT OF TRUTH, SWORD OF THE SPIRIT, AND HELMET OF SALVATION

How many hours do you spend watching television? Americans watch a dizzying amount of TV each day, averaging more than 7 hours and 50 minutes per household. That's equivalent to watching television for three months solid during the year without taking a break! It's a huge distraction and time-waster which the Devil loves because it keeps people from spending time with God and sharing His love with others. It also directly affects your mind in the way you think and act.

The writers of television shows today have an agenda to promote evil in the name of entertainment. These shows are full of crime, violence, hatred, sexual impurity, and mocking of God. Over time, this defiles your mind and dulls your conscience as sin is portrayed as completely "normal and acceptable." To watch, laugh at, and enjoy the evil things on the screen from which God has redeemed you is dishonoring and offensive to Him.

If you want to be in close fellowship with God and prepared for the lies and deception of the world, fill your mind with the truth found in God's Word. What if you spent the same amount of time reading and meditating on the Bible as you did watching television? How incredibly strong your mind would be to fight against all of the world's lies continually coming at you!

Above all else, guard your heart, for everything you do flows from it.

Proverbs 4:23

To guard your heart means to fill it with truth so you can live in a way that glorifies God. You need daily time in God's Word, the *sword of the Spirit*, so that His truth will surround you like a belt.

Go a step further and memorize Scripture so you can be wise with good judgment and discernment when Satan, "the father of lies," tries his best to deceive you. Your one offensive piece of armor for protection, the sword, will not stay sharp on its own. You must continually sharpen it by being in the Word every day.

For the word of God is alive and powerful. It is sharper than the sharpest two-edged sword, cutting between soul and spirit, between joint and marrow. It exposes our innermost thoughts and desires.

Hebrews 4:12 NLT

Along with the *belt of truth* and the *sword of the spirit*, you also need the *helmet of salvation* to be buckled on tightly to fight against the battle for your mind. The helmet protects your head which is where you struggle with thoughts of despair and discouragement.

Do not conform to the pattern of this world, but be transformed by the renewing of your mind. Then you will be able to test and approve what God's will is—his good, pleasing and perfect will.

Romans 12:2

When your mind is focused on the Good News in God's Word, you can easily discern between spiritual truth and spiritual deception. It takes renewing your mind each day by reading the Bible consistently so God's truth can wipe out the enemy's lies, dark thoughts, and confusion from your mind.

ARMOR FOR THE BATTLE FOR YOUR HEART: BREASTPLATE OF RIGHTEOUSNESS

A breastplate is the front portion of plate armor covering the torso, protecting vital organs such as the heart from injury. For defense, we are to put on the *breastplate of righteousness.*

When you repent of your sin, God forgives you, cleanses your heart, and makes you righteous, free from guilt and sin. But when you give in to sin without repenting, you are removing your breastplate and leaving your heart open to the enemy's attacks.

Over time, the more you sin without remorse, the more your heart will begin to harden against God, giving in to the Devil's schemes that he devises to try to keep you as far away from God as he can.

These schemes often come in the form of temptation. It's one of his favorite schemes because it often works. The enemy realizes that as long as you are walking with God and are effective in sharing Christ's message of hope to others, you are a big threat to him.

An easy way to keep you from being effective is by enticing you to sin, tempting you with what you deeply crave, covet, and desire. If you give in, whether it is from drinking too much alcohol, overeating, spending beyond your means, or having sex outside of marriage, it can be devastating and wreak havoc on your life.

What do you crave, covet, or desire that has caused you to battle temptation?

James gives a good warning to Christians:

Temptation comes from our own desires, which entice us and drag us away. These desires give birth to sinful actions. And when sin is allowed to grow, it gives birth to death.

James 1:14-15 NLT

Here is a prayer of protection for your heart:

Teach me your decrees, O Lord; I will keep them to the end. Give me understanding and I will obey your instructions; I will put them into practice with all my heart. Make me walk along the path of your commands, for that is where my happiness is found. Give me an eagerness for your laws rather than a love for money! Turn my eyes from worthless things, and give me life through your word.

Psalm 119:33-37 NLT

Resisting temptation and sin start with the heart. When you guard your heart, filling it with the truths found in God's Word and applying them to your life through obedience, it will be protected by the breastplate of righteousness.

ARMOR FOR THE BATTLE FOR YOUR SPIRIT: FEET FITTED WITH READINESS FROM THE GOSPEL OF PEACE

Back when the Apostle Paul was alive, the shoes worn by the Roman soldiers were called *caligae*. They were specifically designed for long marches with three layers of leather which were pulled up and laced around the ankle. The caligae helped protect the soldiers' feet and also gave them a firm footing for uneven terrain as small spikes or iron hobnails were driven into the soles of the shoes (think *football cleats*).

The enemies of the Roman Empire would place sharp spikes on the ground in front of them before a battle. If an attacking soldier was not wearing shoes that were sturdy enough, he could wind up crippled or killed.

Your feet need to be prepared for spiritual battle. What does it mean to have your *feet fitted with the readiness that comes from the gospel of peace?*

The word *readiness* implies being continuously vigilant and to have your feet firmly planted so you can hold your ground whenever you are attacked. There is a battle going on for your spirit. When the Devil shoots arrows of fear and doubt in your direction, you can be confident that you belong to Jesus Christ because of the gospel – the Good News that He saved you from your sin by taking the punishment that you deserved so you can be with Him forever in your eternal Home.

The gospel of peace allows you to walk on the roughest terrain through the most painful trials in life without fear, knowing what awaits is greater than anything that causes you to suffer in this life. God is your firm foundation!

In addition to standing your ground, shoes are also to be used for walking. God wants you to spread the gospel of peace to others so they can also hear and know the Good News.

When Jesus was encouraging His disciples with a message of hope, He said:

"I have told you these things, so that in me you may have peace. In this world you will have trouble. But take heart! I have overcome the world."

John 16:33

Satan will try to place as many sharp obstacles as he can on your path to keep you from sharing God's plan of freedom. He would love nothing more than for you to stay in the darkness with him. So, be ready for battle by putting on your sturdy, protective shoes each day.

Always be prepared to give an answer to everyone who asks you to give the reason for the hope that you have.

1 Peter 3:15b

SHIELD OF FAITH

The Roman shield in Paul's day was referred to as a *scutum*. It was rectangular, made of wood covered with leather, very large, and quite impressive. Because of its slight curve, it was better able to deflect attacks. Back then, arrows were dipped in oil, lit, and then shot at the enemy. The shields were vital for protecting the soldier from getting burned.

The shield of faith is a protective barrier used to extinguish all of the fiery arrows shot at you by the Devil to try to challenge your faith. Without a strong faith, darts of doubt can penetrate your spirit, wounding you even to the point of causing spiritual death where you no longer believe in God. Faith recognizes the deception and immediately blocks those arrows.

Faith is having complete trust and confidence in God. When you believe in God's character – who he says He is, and believe in His promises – that He will do what He says He'll do, you are demonstrating true faith.

Your faith is strengthened when you spend time in prayer, read and memorize God's Word, and fellowship with others who have a strong faith in God. You remain grounded in truth and the challenges hurled at you by the enemy lose their power. Your faith becomes your shield.

Now faith is confidence in what we hope for and assurance about what we do not see.
Hebrews 11:1

How strong is your faith right now?

How much time do you spend with God in prayer and in reading and memorizing His Word?

Do you see a connection between the strength of your faith and how much time you spend with God?

The shield of faith can also be used to help others. The Roman soldiers had a strategy of joining their shields together in a rectangular shape when the enemy would begin firing at them. Those in the middle of the rectangle would raise their shields over their heads to provide added protection for everyone from airborne weapons.

If you join your shield with others who have a strong faith in God your faith can be strengthened as well, allowing you to more easily take on those destructive missiles aimed at you.

So humble yourselves before God. Resist the devil, and he will flee from you.

James 4:7 NLT

What are the six pieces that make up of the armor of God, necessary for full protection to defeat the enemy?

Know that you never have to fight your spiritual battles alone. God is always with you, protecting and strengthening you with His power so you can live in victory regardless of the enemy's strategy. God's Word tells us when you resist the enemy he has no choice but to run away!

THE GIFT OF VICTORY FOR A RADIANT LIFE

Put on the full armor of God each day so you can stand firm and victorious against the defeated, powerless enemy while you live the radiant life God planned for you in boundless freedom through His gift of victory!

Dear Heavenly Father,

Thank You for the gift of victory. What an encouragement to my soul to know You can use my sufferings for something good. Whenever I go through difficulties, please help me to release any thought patterns of bondage so I can experience victory in every area of my life.

Thank You for the armor of God that I am able to put on for protection from the enemy. I pray that I would guard my heart by obeying Your instructions found in Your Word and not fall into temptation. Thank You for giving me the strength I need to fight these battles and win so I can live in freedom.

In Jesus' name,

Amen

TAKE ACTION

Look back to past abrasives in your life and journal the ways God has used your sufferings for your good and perhaps even for a new purpose.

Put on the full armor of God each day by meditating on the truths found in His Word. You will be able to fight the greatest challenges that come your way so you can win the battle against the enemy.

JOURNAL

LESSON TEN

OCTOBER'S BIRTHSTONE: TOURMALINE
The Gift of Uniqueness

LESSON TEN
October's Birthstone: Tourmaline - The Gift of Uniqueness

KEY VERSE FOR A RADIANT LIFE

For we are God's handiwork, created in Christ Jesus to do good works, which God prepared in advance for us to do.

Ephesians 2:10

YOUR UNIQUENESS, GOD'S GIFT

I was born an October baby. I love the season in which I was born, but I cannot say I feel the same way about my birthstone the opal. Although opal comes in a variety of colors, I have only seen the extremely pale version with very little color displayed in jewelry settings. I am attracted to color, and lots of it, so I have never had a desire to own any opal jewelry.

It was not until just recently that I discovered some great news. October has another traditional birthstone called *tourmaline*.

OCTOBER'S BIRTHSTONE

What an exciting moment this was for me, especially when I found out tourmaline is the most colorful of all gemstones! It occurs in blue, red, green, yellow, orange, brown, pink, purple, white, gray, black, and even multi-colored!

The name *tourmaline* comes from the Sinhalese words *tura mali* which mean "stone of mixed colors." Every piece of tourmaline is unique because of its incredible color variation with no two stones having the exact same color and also because it is pleochroic, appearing to have different colors or depth of color when viewed from different angles. It is important for tourmaline gemstone cutters to consider this before they begin cutting so the finished gem can magnificently reveal its color, transparency, and brilliance.

The group of minerals of which tourmaline is composed can be found in two kinds of rocks: igneous which is solidified from lava and metamorphic, changed in form by heat and pressure. Tourmaline is very unique in that it crystallizes into a three-sided prism which is completely different from any other common mineral.

Elements such as iron, aluminum, magnesium, sodium, lithium, and potassium determine a mineral's color. Tourmaline comes in every color of the spectrum with each colored stone given a different name. For example, blue tourmaline is known as *indicolite*. Today, they are all generally referred to as tourmaline with the color's name added as a prefix.

Tourmaline is primarily mined in Brazil and Africa. Other countries where it is also mined include Afghanistan, Sri Lanka, and in the U.S. in Maine and California. During the early 1900s, these two states were the world's largest producers of gem-quality tourmaline.

Tourmaline became a part of the commercial gem industry when an American mineralogist named George Frederick Kunz walked into the offices of Tiffany & Co. in New York City in 1875. He had with him a beautiful piece of green tourmaline that he had obtained in Maine.

Tiffany & Co. was the largest jewelry business in the world and strictly sold precious gemstones (diamond, ruby, emerald, and sapphire). That day, Kunz was able to meet with the founder, Charles Tiffany, and convinced him to buy his semi-precious tourmaline. That was the very beginning of a long relationship. Eventually, Kunz became the resident gem expert at Tiffany & Co., an influential position that he held for 53 years.

Today, the value of the 100+ hues of tourmaline ranges in price. The more common forms in the colors of pink, red, green, blue, and multi-colored are fairly inexpensive while the rarer, more exotic colors command a much higher price.

Highly sought-after colors include an electric blue-green known as *Paraiba* tourmaline from Brazil, a vivid green called *chrome* tourmaline from Africa, and a tri-colored variety known as *watermelon* tourmaline in which the crystals may be green on one end and pink on the other or green on the outside and pink on the inside.

JULIANA "TOURMALINE"

One of my favorite costume jewelry companies is Juliana because of their unique designs and the color combinations that they used. Not long ago, I purchased a pair of 1960s Juliana vintage clip earrings that resemble watermelon tourmaline.

I repurposed one of the earrings into a striking, colorful ring:

DeLizza and Elster (D & E), the company who created these clip earrings, used paper hang tags to mark their pieces after they changed the name to Juliana in 1967. Without a hang tag, it would normally be impossible to know it was a Juliana piece. However, there are characteristics about their pieces that are completely unique to them, so there are actually several distinctive ways to determine their authenticity.

YOU ARE UNIQUE

Tourmaline is truly a gemological wonder with uniqueness in the color of each piece. You are also an incredible creation and completely unique. Yes, you are a human being made with a physical body and a soul like everyone else, but you are totally unique in your own way.

Part of that uniqueness is the skills with which you were blessed. Each one of us is given unique gifts – special talents or natural abilities to be able to do something well in a way that no one else can. They are a generous gift to you from God.

What are some of your skills that make up your uniqueness?

Every spring, Michael and I attend a huge art festival in Dallas. We always enjoy meeting many talented artists. There are several painters and sculptors, but not one of them creates their art exactly like another. Each artist has their own unique style.

One of the artists we met had picked wild cattail reeds in her hometown of Ohio, colorfully painted them, and then framed her unique art to sell. It was so beautiful. I have never seen anything like it!

GOD HAS A PLAN FOR YOUR SKILLS

Did you know God has had a specific plan for you to be able to use your skills even before you came into the world? That is one of the big reasons why you are here. He wants you to use your skills – your unique gifts – not just for yourself but to bless others, receive joy, and reflect His glory.

For we are God's handiwork, created in Christ Jesus to do good works, which God prepared in advance for us to do.

Ephesians 2:10

How does it make you feel to know that God has specific things prepared for you to do for His glory?

I have had people tell me they do not think they are good at anything. God blesses each one of us with some kind of a skill we can use to serve Him. Sometimes, discovering your unique gifts is a matter of finding what comes naturally to you.

Are you a good cook? Can you write well? Do you like to dig in the dirt and plant beautiful flowers? Do you have an eye for interior decorating? Are you a good listener? All of these, along with many others, are skills that you can use in some way to glorify God.

What are some of your deepest passions that bring you joy?

Why are you given unique gifts? One reason is that God desires for you to experience joy while reflecting His glory. Easily done when you are doing something you love using the talents He has given to you!

Another reason is so that you can use your gifts to show love to others for people to see the love God has for them through you. We have all been given different gifts that are meant to be used for serving others. This is how we show love.

You may have the gift of hospitality. Or perhaps you have the gift of leadership. Maybe encouraging others comes easily for you. Whatever your gifts are, they can and should be used to serve others humbly and to the best of your ability.

What are some of your gifts that you have been able to use to show God's love to others?

These are gifts from God that should not be taken for granted and hidden away, never to be used. Instead, they should be put into practice whenever possible, giving you more opportunities to serve others.

You are a living, breathing instrument employed by God and appointed by Him to do the work of loving and serving others through the incredible gifts He has given you. That is a huge responsibility and one you should never take lightly.

This is how one should regard us, as servants of Christ and stewards of the mysteries of God.

1 Corinthians 4:1 ESV

It can be a complete mystery how sharing your gifts will affect a person's decision in coming to know Christ. But God knows how it all works and He is entrusting you to be a good steward of those gifts.

A BLESSING BEYOND BELIEF

My sister, Heidi, and her family had recently moved to Colorado Springs from Nashville. Before they left, she packed her wiggly, cracked, and fabric-stained kitchen chairs onto the moving truck where they were soon to be unloaded into her new home. She was hoping they would quickly be repaired after the move. But with four young boys, it was not likely that would be happening any time soon.

After living there a couple of months, Heidi met a woman in her new church where her husband was one of the pastors. Heidi mentioned to her that she was wanting to paint her mantle but was not an expert painter. This woman recommended contacting someone in the church named Marisa who owns a creative painting business. Heidi wasted no time and texted Marisa who responded by saying she would love to paint her mantle as a housewarming gift. How incredibly welcoming!

Marisa came over to Heidi's house to help her decide on a paint color and noticed several dismantled chairs in the kitchen. Heidi had somehow found the time to take the first step toward repairing her chairs by purchasing square pieces of wood in hopes of remaking the seats. However, the seats would not fit until the angles could be cut as well. So there they were in several pieces on the floor.

When Marisa saw the seatless chairs along with all of the squares of cut wood she asked, "Would you like me to reupholster your chairs as well? What kind of fabric would you like? Do you like vintage? And are the chairs wiggly? I can fix that, too." As it turns out, Marisa's husband loves to work with wood and had the perfect saw for the job.

If that wasn't enough, upon walking through Heidi's dining room she saw her other set of rickety, stained chairs and offered to paint them a pretty turquoise and reupholster them, too! Within a few days, she was unloading the first beautiful set of chairs from her car and setting them up in Heidi's kitchen. She told Heidi she planned to deliver the other set of chairs in the next few weeks and, of course, her mantle was beautifully painted as well.

Marisa used her unique skills with which God blessed her to bless someone else – a person she hardly knew. It made a tremendous impact on helping my sister feel so welcome in this unknown place where she knew very few people. And it brought her so much joy to have her chairs beautifully repaired by someone who generously shared her talent.

Those chairs would be used in the days ahead to bless many others as Heidi would be hosting multiple families from her neighborhood and her church with the meals she'd be serving around her table.

DISCOVERING YOUR UNIQUE GIFTS

Perhaps you don't have any idea what your unique gifts could possibly be. As God's Word says, we all have gifts given to us for the purpose of being able to use them to serve others. If you are having a difficult time figuring out what your gifts are, ask God to reveal them to you. And He will.

Here are a few tools you can use to help you discover your gifts. Write down what comes to mind as you read through each of these...

TRAVEL BACK TO YOUR CHILDHOOD

Think back as far as you can to the days even before you started school when you were fearless. What kinds of activities did you do that created the greatest memories? What do you remember having the most fun doing? How can you reinterpret this to correlate with your life as an adult? That just might be one of your unique gifts.

LOSE TRACK OF TIME

Have you ever become so involved in an activity that you completely lost track of the time? Was it when you were hard at work or were you engrossed in an enjoyable hobby that took your mind away from the clock? Perhaps that might give you a clue about your natural gifts and abilities.

ASK CLOSE FRIENDS AND FAMILY

People who know you best are able to observe you differently than you can observe yourself, often with much greater clarity than your own self-analysis. Ask close friends and family what they believe might be some of your greatest strengths and talents. They might able to lead you in the direction toward figuring out your gifts.

SPEND TIME WITH YOURSELF

Take time to be alone without any distractions. Whether you only need a few hours or an entire week, it is important to have time to think in the quiet, journal your thoughts, and spend time talking to God and listening to Him speaking to your heart.

Once you know your interests, strengths, and natural talents that make up your gifts, it is important to ask God for direction so you will know where you can use them best to serve others.

He has already had it planned out well ahead of time and will provide plenty of opportunities for you on your journey through life to bless people using your gifts so they can experience God's love for them.

YOUR SKILLS ARE GOD'S GIFT TO YOU

The word *grace* comes from the Greek word *charisma*. Wikipedia defines charisma as "a divinely conferred power or talent." When you are given a skill or talent, that is God's grace – His gift to you. He knows how much blessing and joy you will receive when you use your unique skills to serve Him. You are doing what you are created to do for God's purpose and for His glory.

To improve your talent, learn from others who are skilled at what you love to do. Find a mentor or take lessons from a professional. Sign up to take a few classes to help you become even more skilled at your gift. You never know how God will want to use it to show His love to others through you and bring Him glory.

My friend's high school-aged daughter loves to cook. Everything she makes is gourmet and absolutely beautiful in its presentation. She is a natural at it but desires to learn so much more.

This past summer while staying in Colorado, she asked if she could work without pay at a recreational cooking school. She wanted to learn from professional chefs who could pass their culinary knowledge on to her and, best of all, how to use all of the fun, fancy equipment.

So they put her to work (including washing the dishes), gave her an education, and she came away with much more knowledge about her passion. She currently uses her talent whenever she has an opportunity to cook or bake for her friends and family. It'll be exciting to see how God uses her gifts to bless others in her future!

Just like the gemstone tourmaline, you are truly unique. God chose to give you specific skills for the exact work He planned for you even before you took your first breath.

Be open to all He has created you to do so you can be an incredible blessing to others while receiving abundant joy as you carry out His unique and fulfilling purposes for your life.

DESIGNED TO BE CREATIVE

Do you have a favorite color? We all seem to have personal reactions to different colors as they stimulate our brains in very specific ways.

My favorite has been orange for as long as I can remember. It brightens my mood whenever I see it. Orange is an energetic and fun color which I love to wear, especially during the summer months.

While tangerines, oranges, clementines, and sweet potatoes are all naturally orange, they represent something deeper. As excellent sources of vitamin C, we have come to associate these plant-based foods and the color orange with life and energy.

Psychologically, orange combines the energy of red and the cheerfulness of yellow. Not surprisingly, orange is associated with creativity – the act of using your imagination to come up with new ideas and turning them into reality. I know that when I am able to use my creativity, I have a high amount of energy flowing through me and a definite sense of cheerfulness as I am getting to do what I enjoy.

Home improvement retail giant The Home Depot has been nicknamed "Big Orange" because of the enormous orange sign displayed in the parking lot of their stores. They inspire creativity even with young children, providing free Kids Workshops every month across the country.

Kids get a free project kit for the workshop, a certificate of achievement and pin for a job well done, and a kid-sized orange apron with the words: Build. Learn. Create.

THE DOMINANT BRAIN THEORY

Perhaps you do not consider yourself a creative person. Up until just recently, I did not think everyone could possibly have the gift of creativity. I viewed people as either left-brain or right-brain dominant.

The theory is that left-brain dominant people are those who think in a way that is analytical, linear, and methodical. Those who are more artistic and imaginative with a less organized way of thinking are right-brain dominant.

A team of neuroscientists from the University of Utah tested the theory that people have a dominant brain. In 2013, they found after a two-year analysis that the magnetic resonance imaging of 1011 people, ages 7 to 29, showed there was no proof of this theory. Although the two sides of the brain function differently, they are always working together. No matter how we think, we are all wired to create.

THE PURPOSE FOR OUR CREATIVITY

God made us in His image. As the King of creativity, the One who made the heavens and the earth out of nothing, He designed each of us to be creative just like Him.

So God created mankind in his own image, in the image of God he created them; male and female he created them.
Genesis 1:27

Why is it so important to God that every one of us has the gift of creativity?

People have not been put on this planet to live exclusively for themselves. God has a purpose for us to represent Him in a special, unique way. When we creatively use our gifts, it brings Him glory, especially when we are using them to bless others.

I remember on the day of my wedding feeling very blessed by the creativity of my girlfriend Carol Ann whom I met many years ago in kindergarten. My faithful friend arrived in Dallas all the way from Oregon, ready to help me any way she could.

God gave her the gift of delegating and she also had a creative eye for arranging food in a beautiful, appealing way. It wasn't long before she had my friends and family all working together in the kitchen in a very orderly fashion to have the food ready for the reception immediately following my wedding ceremony.

It was a huge job, but Carol Ann seemed to pull it off with ease. Through her creativity, she made everything look as if it were professionally catered. What a gift she was to me that day!

MADE TO CREATE

It's easy to sit back and do nothing with our creative juices, but it is up to us to discover them and then use them! I have a big sign in my home office that spells out the word CREATE. Each letter is a different size, shape, and material. I purposely hung it on the wall above my desk to remind me to use the energy God gave me to find new ways to create for His glory.

I do this mainly through my writing and making jewelry but also through my vocation as a fitness trainer and water exercise instructor, designing new workout programs with creative exercises for my clients and classes.

Creativity is definitely hard work. It requires perseverance and commitment. Yes, it is much easier to be lazy and not create anything at all – to simply be a consumer of other people's creations. But God did not make us to sit around and do nothing. That would surely suffocate our God-given creative gifts!

Never be lazy, but work hard and serve the Lord enthusiastically.

Romans 12:11 NLT

John Piper wrote about this in his book *Don't Waste Your Life*:

> God has not created us to be idle. Therefore, those who abandon creative productivity lose the joy of God-dependent, world-shaping, God-reflecting purposeful work.

There is great joy in using your creativity to produce your ideas into reality. God has blessed you with the creative ability to reflect His image and bring Him glory. And, in turn, to bless others around you by not wasting or hoarding your gifts. When you use what He has given you, it greatly pleases God.

You have gifts that no one else has. Even with 7.8 billion people in this world, your gifts and creativity are unique to you. God has made plenty of people on the planet who need your creative gifts. And you need theirs.

In what ways do you like to use your creativity?

WHAT CAN KEEP YOU FROM USING YOUR CREATIVITY?

FEAR

Perhaps you are afraid your ideas will fail. Trial and error is a creativity-essential. Dr. Dean Keith Simonton, a Distinguished Professor of Psychology at UC-Davis who studies creativity, found that the more ideas creators come up with, the greater their chances are of producing an eventual masterpiece.

Thomas Edison, described as America's greatest inventor, produced over 1000 patents including the phonograph, motion picture camera, and the electric light bulb. Edison learned much from many of his failed experiments. He admitted, "I make more mistakes than anyone else I know, and sooner or later, I patent most of them."

When Edison died in 1931, he left 3,500 notebooks behind which contained all the details of his many ideas and thoughts. He constantly kept his creative juices flowing!

LACK OF DESIRE

Maybe you have no motivation to be creative. It takes energy, determination, and perseverance to challenge yourself to think creatively. You may simply lack the desire. It is definitely a conscious choice you make to use it or lose it.

Regular practice using your creative imagination is important if you want to keep it. According to a study of 350 children, conducted between 1959 and 1964, kids' natural tendency to daydream and wonder declines sharply around the fourth grade. By the time you are an adult, you become quite constrained by your thought patterns, comfortable in your thought techniques that require little effort or imagination. As Picasso said, "Every child is an artist. The problem is how to remain an artist once we grow up."

God made you to thrive when you use your creativity. If you never use it, how can you possibly live life to the fullest in the way God intended? If you are a follower of Jesus Christ, you will want to please Him in all you do including using, not stifling, your creativity through the gifts He has given you to bless others for His glory.

NO TIME

Perhaps your life is so crazy busy that you cannot imagine taking time out of your ultra packed schedule to think creatively. The good news is that inspiration is all around you in nature. Such a generous gift from our Creator!

Creative thinking can happen naturally if you take time throughout the day just to let your mind wander without any external noise - no phone, no music, or people talking to you. Just a little alone time in the quiet of nature where you have the freedom to let your imagination and creativity run wild.

Set aside time to brainstorm and allow your mind to imagine the seemingly impossible. It is absolutely necessary to take time out of your busy, hectic life to be able to think creatively.

What excuse keeps you from using your creativity?

I now understand why I have always been so drawn to the color orange. Using my creativity keeps life fun and interesting and gives me a reason to jump out of bed in the morning with renewed energy.

Every day is an exciting opportunity to see how God can use your gifts through the creative ideas He gives you. Put aside your fear, get motivated, and find some time in your busy schedule to be creative…the way you were designed to be by the One who's imagination is limitless!

BANISH BOREDOM WITH YOUR UNIQUE GIFTS

"I'm feeling a bit bored lately." I had just overheard the lady in front of me talking to the cashier at the checkout counter in the grocery store.

I wish it would have been an appropriate time to ask her to join me for a cup of coffee right then and there so we could discuss her real reasons for boredom. All I could figure was that she must not know what incredible gifts she has been given by God to share with those around her!

BE ALERT

The Devil absolutely loves it when people are bored. It means they are not pursuing the plans God has for them. They are aimless, living a life that is basically self-centered, not living to serve others. Their talents are wasted along with precious, limited time.

Boredom has got to be one of the Devil's favorites in his toolbox of devices used to keep people from sharing God's love with others while reflecting His glory.

Be alert and of sober mind. Your enemy the devil prowls around like a roaring lion looking for someone to devour.

1 Peter 5:8

To be "alert" means to not give him any chance of catching you off guard. A lion roars when he is very, very hungry. It is at that time when he is the most fierce, eagerly seeking his prey.

If you allow boredom to become a part of your life, that gives the enemy a good opportunity to "devour" you, keeping you away from doing God's work. If you are able to show God's love to others through serving them with your gifts, they might be drawn to Christ and have a personal relationship with Him. That is one more person the Devil loses to his enemy.

Being a follower of Christ requires serving others. He knows exactly where you are needed most. He will give you the direction you need when you are willing to serve others with your gifts. As you serve, know that you are serving Christ who will reward you with an incredible inheritance – eternal life in God's kingdom!

Whatever you do, work heartily, as for the Lord and not for men, knowing that from the Lord you will receive the inheritance as your reward. You are serving the Lord Christ.

Colossians 3:23-24 ESV

Once you are in eternity, one of your greatest joys will be when you are face-to-face with so many of the people you served and loved on earth as a result of using your unique gifts for God's glory.

THE GIFT OF UNIQUENESS FOR A RADIANT LIFE

God has created you with the gift of uniqueness so you can be a blessing to others using your gifts through serving while receiving abundant joy as you carry out His fulfilling purposes to bring Him glory for a radiant life.

Dear Heavenly Father,

Thank You for the gift of uniqueness. I want to be a good steward of my natural talents for creativity, so please help me find ways to improve my skills and use my unique gifts for serving others, reflecting Your glory.

I pray that I would never allow boredom to become any part of my life as I know my time on earth is short. I ask for Your help in conquering any fears I have of using my skills. Thank You for giving me incredible purpose and joy through my uniqueness.

In Jesus' name,

Amen

TAKE ACTION

Look for opportunities where you can serve others using your unique gifts, perhaps through volunteering with an organization or seeking out a need of an individual. If you are unsure of your skills and talents, jump at the chance to serve whenever possible which might help you discover what you are passionate about as well as the skills that seem to come naturally to you. Allow your imagination and creativity to be free!

JOURNAL

LESSON ELEVEN

NOVEMBER'S BIRTHSTONE: CITRINE
The Gift of Joy

LESSON ELEVEN
November's Birthstone: Citrine - The Gift of Joy

KEY VERSE FOR A RADIANT LIFE

Dear brothers and sisters, when troubles of any kind come your way, consider it an opportunity for great joy. For you know that when your faith is tested, your endurance has a chance to grow.

James 1:2-3 NLT

LASTING JOY THROUGH GOD'S GRACE

World War II had finally ended. Four years later, the German Empire split into East and West Germany. Devastated from WWII, West Germany set out to rebuild the economy through very rapid reconstruction. They experienced what is known as *Wirtschaftswunder* or "economic miracle" throughout the 1950s.

From the late '50s on, West Germany had one of the world's strongest economies. The East German economy also showed some strong growth but not nearly as much as in West Germany.

A large contributor to the success of this huge economic upswing came from increased production and manufacturing of goods such as costume jewelry. The materials they used in making jewelry in West Germany had to be inexpensive due to its struggling economy. They became known for their plastic bead sets, beaded tiered bib-style necklaces, and crystal beaded cluster jewelry. They also produced striking jewelry made of glass, imitating precious gemstones.

West Germany's relations with the U.S. improved and costume jewelry, which grew to become a significant industry, was now a part of international trade.

In November of 1989, the head of the East German Communist Party announced that citizens of the German Democratic Republic were free to cross the border. Communism ended in 1990 and the wall that had been built in 1961 to separate the city of Berlin was torn down. East and West Germany reunited becoming known as Germany once again.

One of the pieces I found in my vintage jewelry collection from the 1950s imitated the beautiful gemstone citrine. When I flipped it over to take a look at the back, I noticed it was marked W. Germany! This is a very special piece of history:

NOVEMBER'S BIRTHSTONE

November's traditional birthstone is citrine, a yellow quartz with its natural color ranging between a yellow and reddish orange. The darker colors in a golden orange hue are considered more rare, increasing the value. The mineral iron determines the color in quartz.

Amethyst, a purple variety, is closely related to citrine. When iron is heated, the iron impurities are reduced resulting in less violet purple colors shown in amethyst and more golden orange colors which you see in citrine. It is quite possible that quartz crystals, which grew naturally as amethyst, turned into citrine by the heat from nearby volcanic activity.

The Gemological Institute of America (GIA) discovered that the largest known transparent faceted gemstone is a citrine a little over 19,500 carats which is equal in weight to about 8.6 pounds!

This yellow quartz found mainly in Brazil was renamed citrine over 450 years ago by a German scientist named Georg Bauer. He was known as "the father of mineralogy."

The term *citrine* was officially adopted in 1556 when Bauer used it in a publication about gemstones and jewelry. The root of the word comes from the French word *citron* meaning "yellow" or the Latin word *citrus* for the color of citrus fruit.

CHOOSING JOY

Have you ever watched a baby taste a lemon for the first time? They scrunch up their face with a look of intense displeasure, not at all happy about having experienced this sour and unexpected new flavor.

We often have that same kind of reaction inside of us when having to deal with an unexpected difficulty that comes our way. It can be a sour experience, but there are essential lessons we learn as we go through it that can build our character and make us stronger.

What unexpected difficulty have you had to go through in your life?

Thankfully, God does not expect us to go through painful trials and heartaches without His help. One of the best lifelines He gives us is joy. We can easily become stuck in our anger, bitterness, or sorrow, but He desires for us to choose joy instead, so we can reflect Him as we exhibit the fruit of the Spirit in our lives.

AN OPPORTUNITY FOR JOY

Last summer, I attended an annual fitness conference to keep up my continuing education credits for my personal training and water exercise business, Custom Fitness. We were given a few breaks throughout the weekend to visit with the vendors and check out the latest exercise equipment, music, clothing, and fitness gadgets in the industry.

During one of those breaks, I met a friendly, young blonde woman named Elena. She spoke with a bit of an accent, so I was curious where she was from. She had a spacious booth with a line of fun, colorful activewear. I immediately noticed the tank tops designed with words of inspiration.

I had a feeling she might have an interesting story to tell, so when I got the opportunity I asked Elena if she could take a few minutes to tell me how her company, Tepuy Activewear, came to be.

Elena was more than happy to share. She took me back to 2003 when she had built a successful clothing manufacturing business in Venezuela. When the country's economy became troubled after the Socialist Movement gained power and people became very poor, often turning to theft to survive, it became dangerous to live there. Her business was burglarized six times in one year!

The following year, she and her husband, Rene, made a plan to flee the country leaving everything behind including her 20 profitable boutiques, sewing machines, and sadly, all of her valuable and much-loved employees.

They ended up in Miami where they applied for political asylum and looked for jobs. After many years of working two or three jobs at a time, giving birth to three daughters, and graduating Magna Cum Laude in fashion at The Art Institute of Fort Lauderdale, Elena and her husband became U.S. citizens.

Elena began sewing again, making sportswear under the name Tepuy Activewear in the garage of her home. She explained to me that *Tepuy* means "the house of God."

I understood exactly why she gave her business that name after I heard the rest of the story…

USING HER TALENT

Elena had a deep desire to teach others about God. However, she wasn't confident enough in her English, so she asked God what she should do. He spoke to her heart saying, "Use your talent!"

That is when she began applying Scripture and inspirational words to T-shirts and tank tops right in the garage of her house.

Some of the phrases on the tanks that I saw included:

Choose joy.
Be the light.
I am fearfully and wonderfully made.

She soon outgrew that space and needed to expand. They ended up moving to Americus, Georgia to establish their new home and business. It took off and they now design, produce, and ship thousands of garments each month.

Looking back, she could see that after going through one of the greatest trials of her life, God used it to give her an opportunity for great joy as she offered her talents to be used by Him for His glory.

Dear brothers and sisters, when troubles of any kind come your way, consider it an opportunity for great joy. For you know that when your faith is tested, your endurance has a chance to grow.

James 1:2-3 NLT

Before I left Elena's booth, I couldn't resist buying a tank top for myself. Printed on the front was the word *Inspire*. Elena's story truly inspired me. When you have the Lord in your life, He will always provide opportunities for joy, even in the midst of your most difficult trials.

BEARING FRUIT

There is a major difference between worldly joy and the joy the Holy Spirit gives us when we belong to Christ. Worldly joy is temporary and quickly comes and goes whereas the Holy Spirit's joy is never-ending. There is always an abundant supply.

As the Holy Spirit works to produce change in our character to be more like Him, the result is being able to see fruit in our lives such as joy, an important attribute of the fruit of the Spirit. Bearing fruit is a part of spiritual maturity.

A STRONG BARRIER

The outer layer of a lemon or citron fruit is called the flavedo or rind. It contains essential oils rich in terpenes which are glands that create a strong barrier against the attacks of insects and microorganisms to keep the fruit thriving on the vine.

If we are to be filled with joy, especially through our trials, we must remain attached to Christ so He can be our strong barrier against the attacks of the enemy who would be delighted to see us not bearing any fruit. When we have a close relationship with God, He gives us abundant joy, even during our most difficult challenges in life.

"I am the vine; you are the branches. If you remain in me and I in you, you will bear much fruit; apart from me you can do nothing."

John 15:5

GOD'S GRACE IS OUR JOY

God deeply desires for us to experience lasting joy through Him. The words *joy* and *rejoice* appear in the Bible over 300 times!

The Greek word for joy is *chara* which is closely related to *charis* meaning "grace" or "a gift." Chara is how we react to charis. We have joy because of God's grace.

Through God's grace, we can be joyful despite our circumstances. The joy of the Lord is our strength to get us through anything we go through in life, no matter how painful.

Have you ever experienced supernatural joy during a very difficult circumstance? If so, how?

When we trust in Jesus as our Lord and Savior, we are given so much grace, completely undeserved, as we become heirs to an inheritance that can never perish. There is no greater joy than that!

All honor to God, the God and Father of our Lord Jesus Christ; for it is his boundless mercy that has given us the privilege of being born again so that we are now members of God's own family. Now we live in the hope of eternal life because Christ rose again from the dead. And God has reserved for his children the priceless gift of eternal life; it is kept in heaven for you, pure and undefiled, beyond the reach of change and decay.

1 Peter 1:3-4 TLB

WORLDLY JOY

Commentator Alexander MacLaren (1826-1910) had a great way of describing the end result of worldly joy:

> The saddest lives are those of pleasure-seekers, and the saddest deaths are those of the men who sought for joy where it was not to

be found, and sought for their gratification in a world which leaves them, and which they have to leave.

He went on to write:

> Many of our earthly joys die in the very act of being enjoyed.

Have you ever experienced a time when you were savoring each delectable bite of your favorite dessert and then got to a point where you could not eat any more of it? Your taste buds were most likely on sugar-overload and it just wasn't nearly as pleasurable anymore. Simply stated, your joy died in the very act of being enjoyed!

Have you ever been disappointed by an experience that you thought would give you so much more joy than you actually received?

LASTING JOY

If all there was to joy was what the world offered, we would have good reason to stay stuck in our anger, bitterness, or sorrow. But lasting joy comes from having a deep relationship with Christ as we live in obedience to Him and experience His great love for us. It is an indescribable joy, difficult to express but easily experienced and, best of all, lasting throughout eternity.

Even when life seems like it is giving you a lot of sour lemons, remember you can have joy knowing your final destiny is to be with Christ in His glorious kingdom for all eternity!

HOW BRIGHT IS YOUR LIGHT?

One of my favorite things to do each day is take a leisurely walk with Michael and our senior Pomeranian, Emma (who prefers to ride in her stroller), as the sun begins to go down. We have a great view of the sunset from our house and can watch it in awe as it paints the sky in vibrant pinks, purples, and oranges while walking up and down the hills throughout our neighborhood.

In addition to the sunset, we always take notice of the landscaping in the front yards of people's homes as we love to get new ideas for sprucing up our own yard.

It was getting near dusk one evening and I noticed that the lights bordering a neighbor's walkway were very dim. I asked Michael why anyone would want dim lights. I thought to myself, *What's the point?* He explained to me that they are solar-powered. On cloudy and rainy days, the sun is blocked, diffusing the strength of the sunlight making them dim.

The lack of sunlight greatly impacts their charging ability. If the solar lights do not receive a full charge for many days in a row due to several cloudy days, it affects the life and efficiency of the battery. However, when the sun finally comes back out again for prolonged periods of time, the batteries charge back up and the lights begin to work at full capacity within a few days.

CHARGING YOUR SPIRITUAL BATTERY

The more time you spend with the Lord studying His Word, making time for prayer, and allowing Him to speak to your heart, the more your spiritual battery is charged up so you can reflect Him brightly. He helps you change inside so your thoughts, character, and actions can be more like His.

It is not instant, however. It's a continual process that intensifies in brightness the more time you spend with Him until you are with Him in eternity.

So all of us who have had that veil removed can see and reflect the glory of the Lord. And the Lord—who is the Spirit—makes us more and more like him as we are changed into his glorious image.

2 Corinthians 3:18 NLT

When others see you as a living example of Jesus, they experience His power through you. When your character and actions reflect Him, they know that Jesus is real. His love is real. His joy is real. The brightness of His glory shines through you.

Know that when you shine brightly in this dark world, you stand out! People will be drawn to you and will want to know what it is charging your battery to make you so radiant. The brightness of your light gives you the perfect opportunity to share Jesus' love and joy with others.

You may be going through a really difficult time in your life right now. Perhaps you've recently lost a loved one. Or lost your job. Maybe you're going through a painful divorce. Or perhaps you've been diagnosed with a long-term illness.

There are so many different things that can happen in life which may make you question how it's possible to keep your light shining bright. Yet, God's Word tells us to always be full of joy, a sure way to keep it bright!

Always be full of joy in the Lord; I say it again, rejoice!

Philippians 4:4 TLB

His joy is the light that shines through us, especially when others can see the darkness of the trials and pain we are going through, yet notice we still have joy. We cannot shine on our own without Him.

To rejoice means we must make a deliberate choice to focus on God's goodness in our lives - the many undeserved blessings we so often take for granted. This produces a heart of thankfulness in us.

The Apostle Paul connects expressing gratitude with being joyful:

Always be joyful. Never stop praying. Be thankful in all circumstances, for this is God's will for you who belong to Christ Jesus.

1 Thessalonians 5:16-18 NLT

When we are focused on being thankful, no matter what we are going through, it takes our attention off of our problems and helps us reflect on God's goodness instead. It takes our eyes off of ourselves and back onto God, reminding us how much we need Him.

One way to keep our focus on being thankful is by practicing gratitude. It is good to begin this practice as soon as you wake up.

What are you thankful for this morning? I can easily make a long list without much effort and I bet you can, too. Here are a few of my own examples of what I am thankful for. See how many you can add to the list…

- Feeling rested when I wake up from my comfy bed
- Hot water for my shower
- My cozy home
- Nutritious food
- My loyal husband, Michael, a constant companion
- My sweet Pomeranian, Emma (my other constant companion)
- A good-running vehicle
- The ability to work and get a paycheck
- Good friends who text me sweet, funny, and encouraging messages throughout the day

The more you find to be thankful for, the more you will naturally be filled with joy. Look for all the little things you can thank God for throughout the day. With practice, you will start to notice even the smallest blessings. When your heart is filled with gratitude, you will shine brighter because there is no room for grumbling!

Do everything without grumbling or arguing, so that you may become blameless and pure, "children of God without fault in a warped and crooked generation." Then you will shine among them like stars in the sky as you hold firmly to the word of life.

Philippians 2:14-16a

Replacing grumbling with joy and thankfulness will lead to a powerful witness for Christ. We are different, so we contrast with the darkness in the world as bright lights. Pure and blameless, who we are as followers of Christ, definitely stands out in a warped and crooked generation of people who have turned away from God and the clear path of His Word.

Just like those lights bordering our neighbor's walkway, you are also "solar-powered." You need the Son to keep your light from growing dim. Stay angled toward Jesus, the brightest Light of all, and He will keep you fully charged to share His radiance with the world.

THE GIFT OF JOY FOR A RADIANT LIFE

The gift of joy is never-ending. Because of God's love for you and your undeserved grace, you can have abundant joy and be filled with gratitude for your many blessings, even during your most difficult challenges. Knowing you have an eternal inheritance with Him provides lasting joy for a radiant life.

Dear Heavenly Father,

Thank You for the gift of joy. I pray that I would find opportunities for joy in the midst of my difficult circumstances so I can brilliantly reflect You with the fruit of the Spirit. Please help me to focus on Your goodness each day for a heart full of gratitude and joy. Thank You for the lasting joy You give me knowing my final destiny is to be with You in heaven for all eternity.

In Jesus' name,

Amen

TAKE ACTION

Think about a challenging situation you are facing right now. Spend some time in deep thought and prayer. Journal how God is showing you how you can have joy through it. Practice gratitude by focusing on your blessings each day. Write them down to keep your heart filled with thankfulness toward the One from whom all of your blessings flow.

JOURNAL

LESSON TWELVE

DECEMBER'S BIRTHSTONE: TURQUOISE
The Gift of Stability

LESSON TWELVE
December's Birthstone: Turquoise - The Gift of Stability

KEY VERSE FOR A RADIANT LIFE

Truly he is my rock and my salvation; he is my fortress, I will not be shaken.

Psalm 62:6

ROCK SOLID STABILITY

Having a sibling who enjoys many of the same things I do makes life so much more fun. My sister, Heidi, and I have shared many of the same interests over the years including writing, speaking, having our own business, and seeing the world. Although we live several states away from each other, we have remained close through conversations by phone and traveling to see each other at least a couple of times a year.

THE MAZER BROTHERS

Like Heidi and me, Joseph and Louis Mazer also shared similar interests. They were part of a large family with five other brothers. They all immigrated with their parents to the U.S. from Russia. Once settled, Joseph and Louis decided to open a business together in 1917, producing shoe buckles in Philadelphia, Pennsylvania.

In 1927, they made the big move to New York City and gave their company the fitting name, Mazer Brothers. Louis was their designer and director. Together, they manufactured moderately priced, high quality, abstract costume jewelry that had the look of fine jewelry with precious stones.

The Mazer Brothers used beautiful Swarovski rhinestones to create this glamorous look. Their pieces were marketed as "Jewels of Elegance." The advertisement in *Harper's Bazaar* in 1948 described their jewelry as "The precious look in fashion jewelry."

Their company continued to produce jewelry despite the fact that Joseph Mazer had left in 1946, along with his son Lincoln, to establish his own costume jewelry company using the mark Jomaz.

Here is a beautiful 1960s Jomaz piece from my collection incorporating that glamorous look of diamonds and gold with a robin's egg blue turquoise center:

DECEMBER'S BIRTHSTONE

Turquoise is the traditional birthstone for December. The name *turquoise* is derived from the French term *pierre turquoise* meaning "Turkish stone." It got its name due to the trade routes that brought turquoise to Europe which came from the mines in Persia (now known as Iran) and then went through Turkey. Venetian merchants often purchased turquoise at Turkish bazaars.

Turquoise is an opaque mineral. The scientific name for turquoise is hydrated copper aluminum phosphate. It is found in stunning hues of blue, bluish-green, green, and yellowish-green.

Turquoise forms when water filters through rocks that contain copper, vanadium, and other minerals. Copper adds blue, chromium or vanadium add green, and iron adds yellow. Mines in the U.S. produce mostly green turquoise because of the high content of vanadium and iron. Blue minerals are quite rare in general, so turquoise has become very desirable especially in the robin's egg blue color which was commonly mined in Persia.

STABILIZED TURQUOISE

Only a very small amount of turquoise that is mined today can be used without some type of treatment. Untreated turquoise is very rare. Less than three percent of all turquoise on the market worldwide is natural! If it is "natural turquoise" it means nothing has been altered. The stones are simply polished and cut before being made into jewelry.

The hardest turquoise is usually found close to the surface of the earth where it has had a chance to dry and harden. When turquoise comes straight from the mine, it's like chalk - too soft, porous, and fragile for manufacturing into jewelry because it can easily break or crumble. It has to be stabilized by chemically altering the stone to harden it so it won't crumble.

An epoxy resin or wax is infused into the porous stone which also keeps the color from changing. Once stabilized, it is then durable enough to be cut and used in making jewelry.

IN INSTABILITY WE TRUST

This world we live in is a lot like turquoise – very fragile and unstable. Even so, we can often find ourselves putting our trust in it. We trust in the "stable" company in which we have worked for years. We trust in our nicely padded "stable" bank account. And we trust in the "stability" of our loyal friends and family. At least for a little while.

Then, all of a sudden something happens to break that trust. The company to which you have given hours and hours of your precious time and energy tells you they are downsizing and your job is no longer. You have an unexpected health crisis and your bank account quickly begins to diminish. And your significant other whom you thought was so loyal falls in love with someone else. All of that so-called "stability" has now crumbled.

What have you experienced in your life that caused your trust to be broken?

STRONG AND UNSHAKABLE

Where do you turn when everything in life seems so unstable?

Elohim, which comes from the Hebrew meaning "strength" or "power," is the first name for God found in the Bible and is used in the Old Testament over 2,300 times! God is described throughout His Word as a strong tower, rock, fortress, and refuge. Exactly what we need when everything around us is crumbling and falling apart!

The name of the LORD is a strong tower; The righteous runs into it and is safe.

Proverbs 18:10 NASB

Truly he is my rock and my salvation; he is my fortress, I will not be shaken.

Psalm 62:6

God is our refuge and strength, an ever-present help in trouble.

Psalm 46:1

When you grow in your knowledge of God, you begin to understand how powerfully strong and unshakable He really is. So different from the world we live in! It becomes much easier to run to Him for your stability when you truly know Him. That is because you can fully trust Him to provide exactly what you need - a dependable place of shelter, protection, and security.

SPEND TIME WITH GOD

If you want to get to know someone, you have to spend time with them. To get to know God, you must spend time in His Word which is how He speaks to you. The Bible is filled with His stable promises and everything you need to know about His steadfast character. He is faithful, unchanging, and completely unshakable.

When things in your life begin to lose their stability, God is right there to hold you steady. There is no reason to fear the instability around you because God is your strong tower, your solid rock, and your safe refuge.

When have you found yourself running to God for your stability in the midst of an unstable time?

Spending time with God also includes talking to Him frequently in prayer by thanking Him for all He does for you and telling Him about your hopes and dreams, your greatest needs, and your deepest desires. As you become closer and more intimate in your relationship with Him, you will be able to experience His deep love for you to the fullest.

Your trust will grow and grow and you will lean less and less on your own understanding of things and start to acknowledge God in everything you do. Soon, you will begin to notice that your hopes, dreams, needs, and desires will change over time to align much more closely with His perfect plans and purposes for your life.

BECOME ROOTED IN CHRIST

A few years ago, Michael and I took a trip to Houston for his 30th high school reunion. Before arriving at the big event, we drove around his old neighborhood. He found the street where he used to live and pointed out his memory-filled home.

In the front yard was an enormous tree that was planted by his family 33 years ago. Back then, it was just a tiny sapling. But by now, it had reached a height far above the roof of the house!

As a tree grows taller, its roots grow deeper and the tree becomes more established. The word *established* comes from the Latin *stabiles*, meaning "firm, steady, or stable." The roots, essential for life, carry water and nourishment to the rest of the tree. The depth of the roots, however, depends on the soil and climate conditions.

As you grow closer to God and become more nourished through reading His Word and spending time with Him in prayer, your roots grow deeper. The more time you spend with Him, the greater your trust becomes in the One who gives you His strength with no need to fear when things become unstable all around you. Similar to when a tree is deeply rooted after many years from when it was first planted, it does not have to fear heat or drought.

"But blessed is the one who trusts in the Lord, whose confidence is in him. They will be like a tree planted by the water that sends out its roots by the stream. It does not fear when heat comes; its leaves are always green. It has no worries in a year of drought and never fails to bear fruit."

Jeremiah 17:7-8

What are some of the benefits of trusting in the Lord and putting your confidence in Him?

OUR SOLID ROCK

In 1834, Edward Mote wrote a well-known hymn about having our stability in Christ. Here is the second stanza of his hymn "My Hope is Built on Nothing Less:"

> When darkness veils His lovely face,
> I rest on His unchanging grace;
> In every high and stormy gale
> My anchor holds within the veil.
> On Christ, the solid Rock, I stand;
> All other ground is sinking sand.

Just like turquoise, when you add a source of true stability you become strong and can resist crumbling from the uncertainties in life. That stability can only be found in Christ alone, your solid Rock. And just like robin's egg blue turquoise, an incredible treasure.

OVERWHELMING PEACE BEYOND ALL UNDERSTANDING

Have you ever gotten to a point in life where you feel completely overwhelmed? Like there is this colossal tidal wave swallowing you and you can't seem to come up for a gasp of air, no matter how hard you try?

Overwhelmed happens when you experience mental or emotional strain from a challenging circumstance. When you feel overwhelmed, you may experience intense emotions such as worry, helplessness, anger, anxiety, or perhaps even a panic attack.

The challenging circumstance for you may be keeping a clean and organized house. It may be staying out of debt by sticking to a budget or making sure all the bills are paid on time. Perhaps it's finding time between working and taking care of your family to take care of yourself by planning healthy meals and exercising so you can feel healthy or lose the extra weight you've been carrying around for way too long.

There are many reasons why you can end up feeling overwhelmed. You know what they are. But God never desires for you to live in a state of worry or anxiety. He wants you to run to Him with whatever it is – even if it's the Mt. Kilimanjaro pile of dirty laundry that you don't have the energy or time to deal with. He cares about all of it!

What makes you feel overwhelmed?

He will take your stress, guilt, inadequacy, and whatever else you are feeling and give you perfect peace. An overwhelming peace. He is your Rock of safety.

From the ends of the earth, I cry to you for help when my heart is overwhelmed. Lead me to the towering rock of safety.

Psalm 61:2 NLT

In order to experience this perfect peace, there are three actions you must be willing to take which are all found in God's Word...

GROW IN YOUR RELATIONSHIP WITH JESUS

Perfect peace comes from knowing Jesus Christ, the Prince of Peace. The more you understand who He is, the more peace He will give you for your mind and spirit as you rest in His goodness, faithfulness, power, and wisdom knowing He is in full control of everything.

You gain that knowledge and understanding of who He is by spending time reading His Word. Everything He wants you to know about Him is in His love letter to you. He greatly desires for you to have His perfect peace so you can fulfill His purpose for your life to be a blessing to others, not just living life focused on all of your stress. He made you for so much more!

Grace and peace be yours in abundance through the knowledge of God and of Jesus our Lord.

2 Peter 1:2

If you set out to seek peace for your mind and heart in the world, you may find that it offers plenty of ideas which may sound pretty good such as meditation, finding an "inner light," incorporating healing crystals, visualization, or even sitting in the "Peace Position." But it is all so deceiving. The world completely ignores the true source of peace which is Jesus Christ.

How have you tried to seek peace through what the world offers?

In John 14:27 (NLT), Jesus said:

"I am leaving you with a gift—peace of mind and heart. And the peace I give is a gift the world cannot give. So don't be troubled or afraid."

The world's peace is dependent on having everything going well and in your favor. But when things are not going well, that "peace" is quickly gone. Having a relationship with Jesus allows you to be able to give Him your heavy burdens of worry and anxiety so you can experience His perfect peace.

What heavy burden do you need to give to Jesus so He can take your worry and anxiety?

Expository preacher and scholar Alexander Maclaren had a deep devotion to Christ and His Word. Every morning at 9 o'clock, he would enter his study to prepare his sermons. Before he started, he would kick off his slippers and replace them with heavy, outdoor work boots so he would be reminded of the hard work he was about to do.

I love his explanation of the kind of peace the world gives…

> The peace that earth gives is a poor affair at best. It is shallow; a very thin plating over a depth of restlessness, like some skin of turf on a volcano, where a foot below the surface sulphurous fumes roll, and hellish turbulence seethes. That is the kind of rest that the world brings.

How grateful we can be for the authentic, lasting peace Jesus gives us when we truly know Him and have a relationship with Him.

KEEP YOUR MIND FIXED ON JESUS

When your mind is fixed on Jesus, it is centered and focused on Him and not on all of your challenging, ever-changing circumstances. You trust Him and you lean on Him with all of your burdens because you know His character never changes. When you trust, you are relying on Him, admitting you are weak and need His strength to keep you steady.

You will keep in perfect peace all who trust in you, all whose thoughts are fixed on you!

Isaiah 26:3 NLT

What do you know about God's character and what will you receive if you trust in Him?

I remember traveling out of the country and being on an over-crowded bus with standing room only. I reached for a sturdy pole near me just as the bus was beginning to take off. I was so grateful for that solid, immovable pole because I would have completely lost my balance and fallen over if I had not had it to hold.

You can never steady your own life except by clinging to something strong and sturdy that will not shift. And that something is Jesus. Everything else is fleeting and unstable, but He is always dependable and unfaltering.

When the big tidal wave of stress and anxiety seems as if it is about to swallow you, simply put all of your trust in Jesus. He will make sure you are securely anchored to Him and He will not let you drown.

The promise of having peace in our lives is one of the deepest longings of the human heart. Yet, we often give in to temptation to find rest and peace in anything other than Jesus. The world makes their options look so enticing.

If you want overwhelming peace in your life instead of overwhelming stress, you must be unwavering in your trust, keeping your mind fixed on Jesus. Don't go back and forth like the waves of the sea between trusting Him and trusting what the world offers in the form of superficial peace. You must be committed to waiting on Him in all of the challenging areas of your life so He can fill every part of your being with that steady flow of genuine peace.

PRAY ABOUT EVERYTHING WITH THANKSGIVING

God is your friend. He wants you to pour your heart out to Him with whatever those worries are that weigh on you, big and small. That is what you would do with a close friend who truly cares about all that is going on in your life, right?

Don't worry about anything; instead, pray about everything. Tell God what you need, and thank him for all he has done. Then you will experience God's peace, which exceeds anything we can understand. His peace will guard your hearts and minds as you live in Christ Jesus.

Philippians 4:6-7 NLT

When He says to pray about everything, He means it! I have had people tell me that God doesn't care to have me share the little things with Him because He can't be bothered with such insignificant matters. That couldn't be further from the truth! If we don't tell Him about the little things, our communication and intimacy are limited and there would be very little of our lives we would tell Him about at all. The trivial things are what our big anxieties are made up of.

Although He already knows every detail of your worries even better than you do, He still wants to hear about them from you. He is a very personal God who desires to have a close relationship with you because He made you and He loves you. It glorifies Him when you ask Him to interact with you in all you are going through. That is what makes your relationship more intimate and personal.

If anything is significant enough to cause the slightest anxiety, it is significant enough for you to talk to God about it. The closer you are in your relationship with Him, the stronger your instinct will be to share the details of your life. Complete openness with God is evidence of a right relationship with Him.

Is there anything going on in your life right now that you think is too insignificant to talk to God about?

The other important part of sharing your anxieties with God is giving Him thanks for the mercies and goodness you have received in your life. You will never run out of things to thank Him for! When you focus on all He has done for you, from providing for your needs here on earth to providing an eternal Home for you in heaven, it offers a calmness to your heart, mind, and spirit and a definite sense of peace.

You cannot expect to fully enjoy future mercies when you are not even thankful for those you've been given in the past and present. Just like when you express thankfulness to someone for doing something nice for you, thanking God is a way of humbling yourself. Your attitude is not one of entitlement but of thankfulness for the undeserved blessings He has graciously poured out on you.

I have been making more of an effort to acknowledge God's goodness in my life by saying, "Thank you, Lord!" whenever I notice something for which to be thankful. I find I am saying it quite a bit because He continually showers so much of His goodness on me! It takes less of a conscious effort the more you thank Him because it begins to become a natural part of your daily interaction with God. This has created a much more grateful heart in me that has led to more peace and less focus on my worries.

Pray about everything, with thanksgiving, so His peace will be a guard around your heart and mind from all anxiety. It cannot be explained or comprehended. You just need to do it and experience it for yourself!

Life is like the ocean with those colossal tidal waves. It can cause so much turmoil on the surface as the waves crash into the shore, yet so much peace if you dive down deep. Much like your relationship can be with Jesus. The deeper you plunge into knowing Him, devoting your time to Him, giving Him your complete trust, sharing the details of your life, and expressing your thankfulness to Him, the more peace you will experience. It's a peace that is overwhelming and goes far beyond all comprehension and understanding.

THE GIFT OF STABILITY FOR A RADIANT LIFE

God is your solid rock, strong tower, mighty fortress, and safe refuge. His character is steadfast. He is faithful, unchanging, and completely unshakable, providing you with the gift of stability in an unstable world so you can experience a radiant life.

Dear Heavenly Father,

Thank You for the gift of stability. I am so grateful I can run to You when things in my life start to crumble. Please help me remember there is no reason to fear the instability all around me because You are my solid Rock. Take all of my stress and anxiety from me so I can experience Your perfect peace. Help me to trust You more and more as I grow closer to You. Thank You that I have nothing to fear with You as my refuge and strength.

In Jesus' name,

Amen

TAKE ACTION

Journal your fears – those things in your life that have no stability. Then, write out the Scriptures listed in the lesson that describe God as a strong tower, rock, fortress, refuge, and strength. Read them out loud each day as a good reminder that true stability can only be found in Him.